Illustrated Football Drills
from The Coaching Clinic

Other Books Compiled by the Editors of <u>The Coaching Clinic</u>:

Best of Basketball from *The Coaching Clinic*—1966

Best of Football from *The Coaching Clinic*—1967

Handbook of Basketball Drills from *The Coaching Clinic*—1972

Illustrated Football Drills
from The Coaching Clinic

Compiled by the Editors of
The Coaching Clinic

Parker Publishing Company, Inc.
West Nyack, New York

Library of Congress Cataloging in Publication Data
Main entry under title:

Illustrated football drills from the Coaching clinic.

   1. Football--Addresses, essays, lectures. 2. Football coaching--Addresses, essays, lectures. I. The Coaching clinic.
GV951.I44   796.33'22   74-28013
ISBN 0-13-451021-6

Introduction

Execution is the key to winning consistency in football—without it even the best offensive and defensive strategies are wasted.

So here are 48 drills from some of the best high school and college coaches in the game, all of them designed to develop the essential individual and team skills that are the backbone of winning football.

Culled from the pages of the monthly publication *The Coaching Clinic*, these drills cover virtually every aspect of football play—from ball-carrying to tackling, from blocking to the kicking game.

Whether you're a novice or a vet, at whatever level of play you coach, this book is certain to become one of your most valuable tools in building a winning football program.

The Board of Editors of The Coaching Clinic

CONTENTS

PART I   OFFENSIVE DRILLS *(Cont'd)*

PART II   DEFENSIVE DRILLS

PART II   DEFENSIVE DRILLS *(Cont'd)*

PART III   SPECIAL DRILLS

PART III   SPECIAL DRILLS *(Cont'd)*

PART III   SPECIAL DRILLS *(Cont'd)*

Part I

OFFENSIVE DRILLS

1

Techniques and Drills for a "Run-to-Daylight" Offense

by David W. Bryan

Head Football Coach

Mainland Regional (Linwood, New Jersey) High School

David Bryan has been coaching football since 1961—Reynolds (Trenton, N.J.) High School; Hamilton (Trenton, N.J.) High School; Oakcrest (Mays Landing, N.J.) High School; Pennsylvania Military (Chester, Pa.) College; Mainland Regional (Linwood, N.J.) High School. His overall coaching record is 73-42-1 and includes a county championship, a division championship, and number-one ranking in New Jersey. The following article is based on his work at Oakcrest High School.

The term "run to daylight" is a popular one, used in conjunction with offensive football—but very little has been written about the development of the skills necessary to run such an attack. I have utilized the offense for the past three years at two schools and it has produced a 23-4 record.

My interpretation of "run to daylight" is to have the offensive lineman block the defensive man in any direction he can and then have the back run accordingly. This concept is the basis of our offense at Oakcrest (Mays Landing, New Jersey) High School.

The two most important factors involved are:

1. The utilization of a blocking technique that offers the desired flexibility;

2. The development of the ability of the backs to "read" the blocks and run to the point of least resistance.

Blocking Techniques

The basic block used is the "numbers block," usually called the "face block." The coaching points of teaching this technique are:

1. *Explosion*
    a. Forehead into numbers of opponent, stepping with right foot. Snap head upward in violent movement, attempting to hit man in chin with top of helmet.
    b. Whip hands upward in violent motion to own chin. Keep

hands clenched together and close to body. Forearms should be parallel to ground and elbows extended outward from shoulders.

2. *Blocking surface*—this is the entire upper body from top of helmet to belt buckle and elbow to elbow.

3. *Turn and shield*—the primary purpose of the numbers block is to turn the man and shield him "right now" in the direction he wants to go. We are not interested in driving him backwards. After we have created a shield, then we can move him laterally.

I feel that this block is successful because we aren't fighting the defensive man. Most defensive linemen are taught to deliver a blow and straighten up the offensive man. In reality we are standing up, but to our advantage. Even if we can't accomplish a shield with our bodies, the opponent himself is upright, with his weight back on his heels, and he will have a vision problem with our helmet in his face.

COACHING POINTS: Keep elbows up; utilize blocking surface. Turn the man in the direction he wants to go—shield. Stay on feet; keep a wide base; make short, choppy steps; keep the hands in. If he starts to slip, scramble, then use a cross-body.

The numbers block is utilized in all phases of our offense —trapping, downfield, pulling, cross-blocking, and double-teaming. We do, however, use scramble, shoulder, and cross-body as well.

Blocking Drills

Very light dummies are utilized in our blocking drills.

1. *Position and shield.* Blocker leans against dummy in a good position and on command revolves around dummy for complete turn—right and left.

2. *Explosion.* From a comfortable three-point stance, fire out, hit with head, snap head up, and bring blocking surface into play. (See Diagram 1.)

3. *Numbers block drill.* Put player in a three-point stance with dummy directly in front of him. On command, player explodes and executes a numbers block. Dummy holder will vary his charge. It is important that he imitates a defensive charge by exerting pressure

Diagram 1

inside, outside, and head up. The blocker must block him accordingly.

4. *Closed eye*. Put player in stance with eyes closed, have dummy holder vary position of dummy. On command, player explodes and opens eyes, and he blocks dummy in the best direction.

5. *Closed-eye pulling*. Two blockers are in a stance next to each other between two dummies with eyes closed. Dummy holders vary dummy position. On command, player executes good pulling technique, opens eyes, locates dummy, and blocks it however he can. (See Diagram 2.)

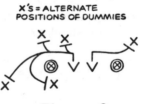

Diagram 2

6. *Length of field*. Have all players line up and each executes a numbers block from his three-point stance, driving the dummy straight back for a distance of 15 to 20 yards.

Backfield Skills

The "run-to-daylight" ability is a skill that very few backs have naturally, but we incorporate two major drills that help develop this ability. Most of our backfield drills are the same ones that most coaches use—sideline, fumble, balance, handoff, etc. I feel, however, that the "closed-eye" drills are original and very productive. The "closed-eye" drills for line and backs originated during a search for practical drills to perform indoors on rainy days.

1. *Closed-eye cut.* All backs line up single file about 12 yards from a dummy. They run straight ahead about one-half speed with eyes closed. There is a player in front of the dummy, between the dummy and the ballcarrier. On command, the ballcarrier opens his eyes and reads the action of the blocker, who slips his head to one side or the other of the dummy. The ballcarrier cuts to the side of the blocker's head, shifting the ball away from the defensive man. (See Diagram 3.)

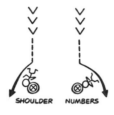

SHOULDER   NUMBERS

Diagram 3

NOTE: As the boys progress they will be able to run faster, and the coach can wait until they are closer to the dummy before he gives the command to open the eyes. This drill can be varied in many ways or incorporated into other drills—closed eye, hand-off, and cut.

2. *Closed-eye multiple hole.* Several dummies are lined up at 4-yard intervals; the back runs parallel to or at a slight angle to the dummies and about 4 yards away. On command, the back plants himself, opens his eyes, and reads where he is in relationship to the dummies. He should run for the nearest opening, hit the hole square, cover the ball, maintain speed, and keep his head up and eyes open, looking for downfield blocks. (See Diagram 4.)

COACHING POINTS: The running back must receive the ball deep in the backfield to have time to read the block and react. Do not slow down, stop, or hesitate when reacting to the block. Shift the ball when

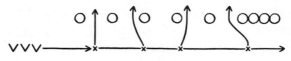

Diagram 4

cutting—don't attempt to straight-arm at the line of scrimmage. Use a forearm lift with free arm or spin. Hit the hole square. Run to the goal line—lateral movement should be kept to a minimum unless the back has exceptional speed.

Offensive Philosophy

The "run-to-daylight" philosophy has been incorporated into a "flip-flop" T formation that utilizes balanced and unbalanced lines.

The basic most successful play of our offense is the dive play. Through the use of the following features, the simple, old-fashioned "strong dive" is run with at least 50 different variations, with no change in blocking assignments.

> NOTE: (1) flip-flop; (2) balanced and unbalanced; (3) backfield motion; (4) backfield "sets"—wing, flanker, etc.; liberal and arbitrary split rules.

Our offensive plays are called by name; i.e., strong dive, weak dive, power play, etc. This takes no more effort or time in the huddle and there is less chance of confusion. Even though some plays have a preferred hole, the advantage of this system is that the backs and line don't get the idea that a predetermined hole has to be run.

> NOTE: The skills described in this article are not instinctive; however, through constant drilling on the fundamentals, this offense will work with boys of any size, is easily learned, and is very difficult to defense.

2

Ideas and Drills for the Flank Attack

by Martin Tullai

Head Football Coach

St. Paul's (Brooklandville, Maryland) School for Boys

Martin "Mitch" Tullai has been head football coach and athletic director at St. Paul's School for Boys since 1953. At last count, his record totaled a 61% winning average. This includes various conference and league championships and an undefeated season in 1970

Last season we had a fine game-tested backfield, but our line was weak in total experience. Consequently, we felt it would be in our interest to devise an offense in which our backs not only carried the ball, but also bore the brunt of the blocking load.

> RESULT: The result was the variegated attack. By this we mean a variety of backs hitting the flank for a number of different backfield sets. The diverse adjustments enable a particular back to be placed in the most opportune position from which to strike at the flank.

These adjustments, of course, do not preclude the use of other series such as "dive," "scissors," "ride," etc. In fact, these enhance the overall attack. Additionally, the passing attack becomes more versatile.

General Information

With a minimum of faking and ball handling, a premium is placed on effective open field blocking. The three backs and the pulling guard bear the brunt of the blocking at the flank. This doesn't mean that they must be huge physical specimens. Last season, using this offense as the heart of the attack, 314 points (a school record) were scored with a backfield averaging 168 lbs. and guards at around 165 lbs. These boys, however, must be steeped in good blocking procedures and must develop a deep sense of personal and team pride.

EFFECTIVE BLOCKING: It's obvious that in offensive football there is no substitute for effective blocking. Not faking, not multiple ball-handling, not trick plays —nothing can bring the high measure of success to a team that sound, tough, efficient blocking can insure.

Pride in blocking: It is paramount to our success to constantly work on building pride in blocking because this is so important a phase of our offense. An opportunity to point out a fine block is constantly sought. Bulletin board pictures show good form and striking poses. While drilling, the well-executed blocks are highlighted—"nice going," "that's a boy," "that's the way to sting 'em," and so forth.

TIP: When scrimmaging, the whistle is blown to freeze everyone to point out a block of substance. When viewing game films a big fuss is made over the boy who threw a key block, and his name and number are enthusiastically pointed out.

The squad should realize the importance of ball carriers and pass receivers, but it is mandatory that they realize that good blockers are the most vital ingredient for success.

Types of blocks: In order to effectively carry out blocking responsibilities, we feel that three blocks must be mastered—the long body block, the reverse body block and the shoulder block. Heavy stress is placed on the long body block. In tight, behind, or on the line of scrimmage, a shoulder block must be utilized to blast the defender out of the area. But in the open field, we like our backs, as well as linemen, to get as close to the defender as possible and throw a tough whiplash type of body block with the on arm swung across the body, thereby providing additional impetus to the blow.

NOTE: Should the execution lack perfection it is of utmost importance to emphasize the necessity of rolling into and through the opponent to harass and maintain contact to prevent his movement to the ball carrier.

Blocking Rules

Our numbering system follows. Linemen as well as backs are numbered. The areas at each flank are also given numbers. Ends are identified with "East" and "West" designations (Figure 1). The wing

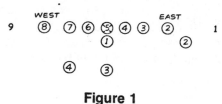

Figure 1

right alignment shown in the figure is one of several possible backfield arrangements. When adjustments are simple, they do contribute to versatility of the offense and hence to the offensive capability.

SERIES: Series are indicated by letters (A, B, X, etc.). For the purpose of this article, the "A" pitch-out or flank series is discussed.

It goes without saying that blocking rules should be as simple and consistent as possible. Furthermore, the interior offensive line is faced with the most trying offensive duties—but very often they are saddled with so many blocking rules and exceptions that they get lost in the confusion. It's tough enough to block the man properly when one knows who it is—but if he isn't sure or is hesitant, the only pay-off is chaos and lost yardage. Consequently, common sense and survival dictate that simple, uncluttered rules should be established.

Since the backs and ends are more involved in the "glory phases" of the game, we feel that it is incumbent upon these boys to accept the responsibility of learning different assignments from play to play. A back might be a ball carrier on one play hitting at the flank, but a blocker on the next. He may lead-block one time, but become the second blocker on the following play. All backs block and all backs carry the ball. In this system, there is a reciprocal factor which promotes harmony among the "four horsemen."

Line rules: The rules for the linemen are as follows.

> *R. E. (2).* Block man head-on; no man head-on, block first man to inside.

> *R. T. (3).* Block man head-on; no man head-on, block first man to inside.

> *R. G. (4).* Block man head-on; no man head-on, block first man to inside. Vs. odd defense (5-4), move downfield after short

drop step behind R.T. Block defensive HB either way, out preferably. However, do not pass up a dangerous opposite color.

C. (5). Block man head-on; no man head-on, fill to your left for the pulling guard.

L. G. (6). Pull and lead. Do not pull too deeply. As soon as the corner is rounded, look to cut off interior pursuit. However, do not pass up a dangerous opposite color behind the line.

L. T. (7). Block aggressively man head-on or to outside for two counts. Then hustle downfield to cut off pursuit.

L. E. (8). Block aggressively man head-on or to outside for two counts. Then hustle downfield to cut off pursuit.

Backfield rules: The rules for the backfield are as follows.

Lead Blocker. Block the first man outside the end. If possible hook him in, but if he moves to the outside, blast him out (this is an option block).

2nd Back Out. Make sure the end is secure. If there is any question as to the defensive end's ability to make the play, blast him. If lead blocker has secured the end, cut upfield quickly and look for opposite color—this should be the rover back or defensive HB.

3rd Man Out (Generally the QB). Do not gain too much depth. Make sure the area behind the line of scrimmage is secure. Turn the corner. Check inside first. If the inside offers no danger, continue upfield, block dangerous color.

Ball Carrier. Receive the ball looking at the QB. Read the ball into your hands. Put it away properly. Run at controlled speed. Cut upfield as soon as the area is secured. If the end is hooked in, run outside. If he is trapped out, cut up inside—it is your option, but you must read the defense and the blocking as you're moving.

NOTE: Once the corner is cleared, it is imperative that the ball carrier run to positive yardage rather than continue his lateral movement toward the sideline. That is, he must cut upfield as soon as the carrier is secured. One cannot assume that high school backs understand this "obvious maneuver"—it must be drilled repeatedly.

An alternate blocking method on the defensive end has proven quite effective. This would have the end and wingback executing an "X" or quasi-cross block. As the wingback crosses first, his movement has a tendency to draw the defensive end in to protect the off-tackle hole. This enables the end to pull outside and effectively hook him (Figure 2).

Figure 2

"A" Flank Series with Varied Backfield Sets

One (1) hole plays are described here, but the same plays are mirrored to the (9) hole. The linemen do not flip-flop, but the backs maintain their same positions. The (2) back is always the wingback and in certain situations a deep halfback. The (3) back is always the fullback. The (4) back is always a deep halfback or the tailback in the "I" formation (Figures 3 through 11).

Counter-Plays

Obviously, continued use of the flank attack is bound to result in adjusted defenses and heavy defense pursuit. To combat this, plays from other series can be run effectively from these sets, or counter-plays designed to take advantage of the defensive weakness can be employed. Several counter-plays which have proven effective for us are as follows (Figures 12 through 14).

Drills

In addition to the standard drills, the following can be useful for the flank attack offense.

1. *Quarterback pitchout drill:* (Figure 15). The purpose here is to

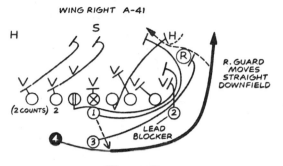

Figure 3

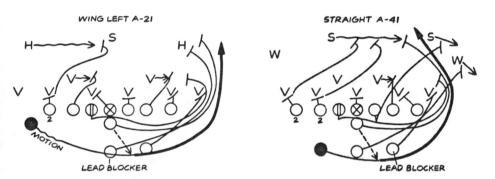

Figure 4

Figure 5

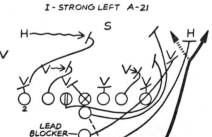

Figure 6

I - STRONG RIGHT A-41

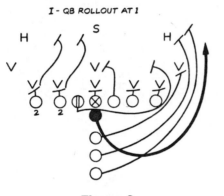

LEAD BLOCKER

Figure 7

I - QB ROLLOUT AT 1

Figure 8

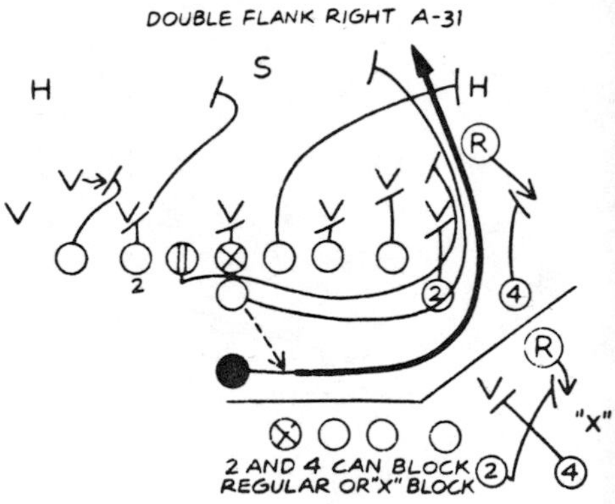

DOUBLE FLANK RIGHT A-31

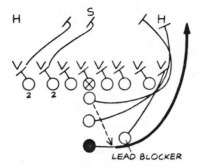

2 AND 4 CAN BLOCK
REGULAR OR "X" BLOCK

Figure 9

I - WING LEFT, WEST OVER A-21

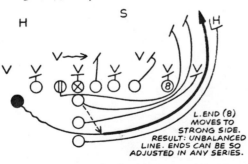

L. END (8)
MOVES TO
STRONG SIDE.
RESULT: UNBALANCED
LINE. ENDS CAN BE SO
ADJUSTED IN ANY SERIES.

Figure 10

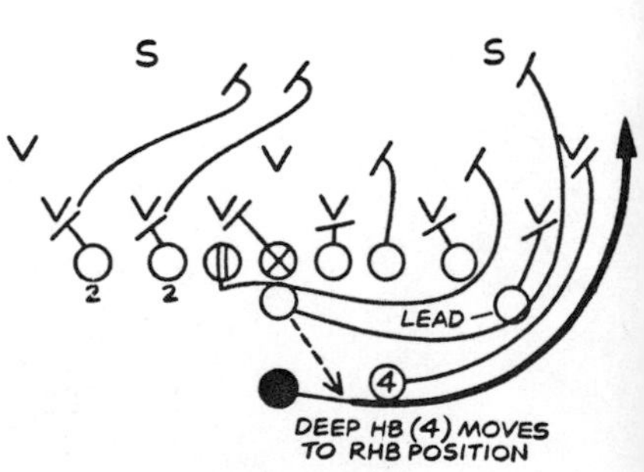

OVERLOAD RIGHT A-31

LEAD —

DEEP HB (4) MOVES
TO RHB POSITION

Figure 11

WING RIGHT 41 QUICK PITCH PASS

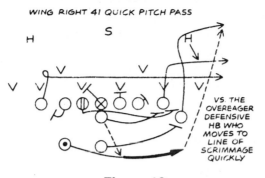

VS. THE
OVEREAGER
DEFENSIVE
HB WHO
MOVES TO
LINE OF
SCRIMMAGE
QUICKLY

Figure 12

WING LEFT - A-46 COUNTER

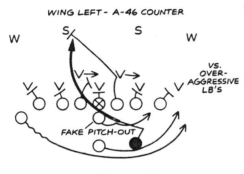

VS.
OVER-
AGGRESSIVE
LB'S

FAKE PITCH-OUT

Figure 13

WING RIGHT - A-29 DOUBLE REVERSE

VS.
WELL-
DRILLED
DEFENSE
SHOWING
GOOD
PURSUIT

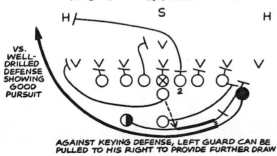

AGAINST KEYING DEFENSE, LEFT GUARD CAN BE
PULLED TO HIS RIGHT TO PROVIDE FURTHER DRAW

Figure 14   **Figure 15**

check the quarterback-center exchange for proper pivot and release.
Also, we want to check reception by deep backs—proper reading of
ball into hands, proper reception and proper carrying. Then, too, we
want the backs to practice going both ways and align in different
positions (RHB, LHB, FB and WB).

2. *Phalanx drill vs. bags:* (Figures 16, 17, 18). For this drill we
set up as shown in the figures. Adjust the bags in various positions
—end out wide, halfback up tight, etc. The purpose is to perfect
backfield blocking and to pick out the proper man. We stress that the
backs get close to the man before throwing the whiplash body block.
We run complete backfields from all sets—three possibilities are
shown in the figures.

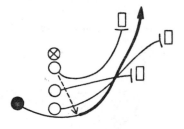

Figure 16

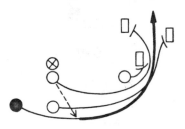

Figure 17

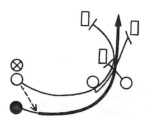

Figure 18

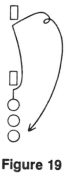

Figure 19

Figure 20

3. *Succession drill:* (Figure 19). In our succession drill, we want to develop second-effort instinct. The players throw the first block (either shoulder or long body block), recover, hustle to second bag, throw long body block, execute roll and recover.

4. *Cutting off a block:* (Figure 20). This drill teaches the ball carrier to properly cut off a block. The ball carrier should throw a fake before cutting.

3

Offensive Backfield Drills

by Jimmy Feix

Head Football Coach

Western Kentucky University

Jimmy Feix was named head football coach at Western Kentucky University in 1967, and in his rookie year led his squad to a 7-2 mark and a tie with nationally ranked and bowl-bound Akron. In six seasons, Feix's teams have never suffered more than three losses in a single year and have never finished lower than second place in an OVC race. His Hilltoppers have won the league title three times, in 1970, 1971, and 1973. Coach Feix's career record to date is 48-12-3 for a winning percentage of .786. His six Hilltopper teams have won 33, lost 8, and tied 1 in conference competition, a .798 percentage.

At Western Kentucky State College, drills to teach and perfect those fundamentals necessary for the overall success of an offensive back are an all-important part of our daily practice schedule. While defensive drills are worked into our schedule on an alternating-day basis, certain selected basic offensive drills are repeated every practice day. Here's why:

1. Offensive maneuvers require more skill and technique.

2. Teaching is more efficient in drill groups than in team groups, because of group size and number of repetitions possible.

3. Neuromuscular patterns and motor learnings are perfected through repetition.

4. Some practice is possible in small coaching staffs under student-athletic direction and supervision.

> TIME-SAVER: To save time, each drill we use has an identifying name. After initial instruction in arrangement and performance, the players recognize what they are to do by the naming of the drill and begin immediately—even without supervision.

The following are fundamental movement drills that serve a wide range of objectives—from teaching beginners proper running and body carriage techniques to improving the reaction, flexibility, power, and balance of the more advanced high school and college player.

DIAGRAM LEGEND: (X) = player with ball; X = player without ball; (B) = player who is to block; (T) =

player who is to tackle; □ = large dummy, standing;
——➤ = path of player; ---➤ = path of ball.

Cross-over run: Players, in turn, run a distance from 20 to 50 total yards from starting line—around a dummy, goal post, or designated line and back to the starting point (Diagram 1). Players should allow from 3 to 5 yards between them. Facing at right angles to direction of movement, they run and swing the back leg alternately in front of and behind the lead stepping leg. The body should be bent at the waist. TIP: Coach for a high-stepping, high-knee action with exaggerated hip pivot.

Backward run: Same organization as in Diagram 1. Players run facing 180° from the direction of movement. TIP: Strive for shoulder and hip-pivoting action as boys reach as far backward with steps as possible.

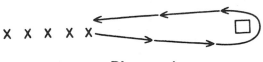

Diagram 1

Spinning: Here we divide the players into two groups as they perform the basic ball-carrier's spin from a tackler. In Diagram 2, every other player spins 90° in opposite directions; in Diagram 3, one group becomes the ball carriers, the other the tacklers. Players switch lines after finishing their turn.

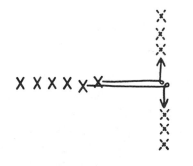

Diagram 2

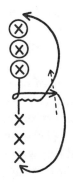

Diagram 3

TIP: Coach ball carriers for head-and-shoulder fake on the "plant" or "cutting" foot, high-knee action in the spin, and 90° change of direction. Players without a ball have knees bent, arms hanging, head-up position. They shuffle to stay in front of the ball carrier. (They are not "live" tacklers.)

Ball exchange: This drill is used to teach all types of ball exchange and fake of exchange (i.e., inside-arm-up give or fake give; palms up as in halfback-to-halfback reverse; flipping of laterals). On command "change," the players begin exchanging ball from side of receiver opposite of that used in the beginning. The command "fake" has the player faking an exchange to the first back he meets in the chain and handing off to the second back he meets. "Reverse" is the command to start the use of the exchange in reverse maneuvers. The command "flip" causes the players to pitch the ball at a distance of from 3 to 6 yards apart (Diagram 4).

Diagram 4

Figure eight: This is an adapted basketball weave drill to develop and perfect change of direction, ball concentration, and handling. As players weave to and from the designated point, the ball is flipped forward (Diagram 5) in the three-man weave. In Diagram 6, the five-man weave, the ball is flipped forward in the beginning by the middle man to the player on either side of him—and thereafter is flipped backward.

Sideline cuts: We use this drill for simulating a game situation in which a ball carrier is angled at the sideline and eludes a tackler with a change of pace or some cut-back maneuver. Groups are about 10 yards apart. The player without the ball cannot start his advance until the player with the ball starts toward the sideline (Diagram 7).

Three-man roll: Each player has a ball and performs the grass drill roll with the ball under his arm. Coach to prevent fumbles caused by hitting the ground. This drill helps backs learn to fall, react, and move with the ball under their arm as a natural part of the body. In Diagram 8, the middle player dives and rolls under the player to his

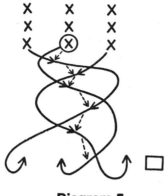

Diagram 5

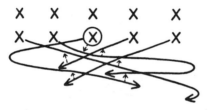

Diagram 6

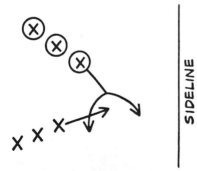

SIDELINE

Diagram 7

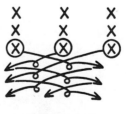

Diagram 8

right and regains his feet. The player to his right dives over the rolling middle player and rolls under the player in the left column who is diving over him.

> TIP: This procedure continues for as long as the coach desires. However, short, snappy drills taking a couple of turns seem more effective than one long turn —unless endurance performance is the objective.

Ball carrier—blocker: This drill incorporates several teaching opportunities—ball carrier moves; downfield blocking techniques; defensive back's playing off of a blocker; open field tackling; etc. As illustrated in Diagram 9, on a whistle signal, the ball carrier and

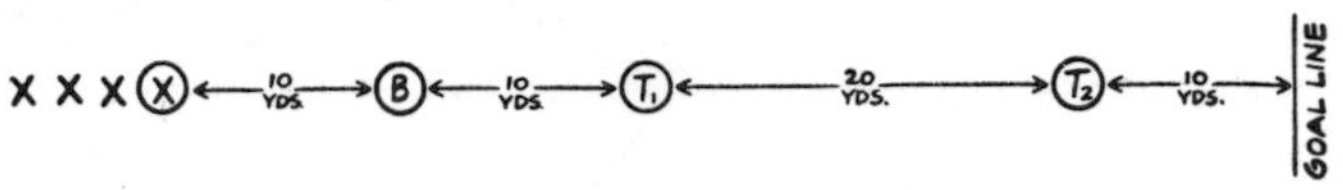

X X X (X)←—10 YDS.—→(B)←—10 YDS.—→(T₁)←————20 YDS.————→(T₂)←—10 YDS.—→ | GOAL LINE

Diagram 9

blocker start toward (T₁) who plays blocker and attempts to make a tackle. After the ball carrier has escaped or been tackled by (T₁) , he attempts to elude (T₂) 's tackle. Blocker goes to the end of the waiting line of players, (T₁) becomes (B) , (T₂) moves up to (T₁) , and (X) becomes (T₂) , as the next waiting player becomes (X) .

4

Skeleton Offensive Combination Drills

by Marv Hiebert

Head Football Coach

Mt. Hood (Gresham, Oregon) Community College

Marv Hiebert became the inaugural head football coach at Mt. Hood Community College in September, 1970. Before moving to Mt. Hood, Coach Hiebert served as head coach at David Douglas High School from 1959 to 1969, where his teams were league champions four years and state champions in 1960 and 1965. His overall coaching record at all levels is 86 wins, 29 losses, and 5 ties.

To develop a ball control offense and defensive reactions simultaneously in a controlled situation, we prefer skeleton offensive combination drills. They provide an opportunity to isolate the area of attack so that mistakes can be minimized.

PERSONNEL: In these drills, we employ various combinations of personnel to achieve our objective —complete backfield and guards working on sweep plays; onside tackle, end, and offside guard pulling in executing a running play; etc.

It's our objective to develop a "power attack" offense based on double team blocking, drive blocking, wedging, trapping, and isolation blocking.

Coaching time: It's a great concern to our staff to organize simple and meaningful drills in which each player receives equal coaching time. Thus, a greater number of players can be developed for varsity competition. It's important that our boys believe the football field is marked off in inches—and that we do not want to lose control of the ball because of a failure to gain the additional inch.

Objectives: The objectives of skeleton combination drills are numerous. Some are as follows:

1. To develop a point of attack at a designated area on the line of scrimmage, allowing coach and players to focus attention on that area.

2. To isolate the team by positions, allowing backs and linemen to work together in perfecting key blocking assignments.

3. To develop offensive and defensive techniques simultaneously under game-like conditions.

4. To recognize different defenses so that our quarterbacks may make the proper calls on offense.

> EXAMPLE: As shown in the variations to the basic drill (Diagram 2), when the defensive secondary is rotating quickly to stop the power sweep, the quarterback should sense that a run action pass would be in order. If defensive tackles are penetrating aggressively across the line of scrimmage, trap plays would be most effective.

5. To provide a controlled learning situation for the defense so that they learn to read the offensive action and react in proper pursuit patterns.

Organization: To implement the drills with a 48-man squad, we have divided the squad into four teams to make it easier to give each player equal coaching time. Each team is designated by a different colored jersey: Blue—1st team; red—2nd team; grey—3rd team; white—4th team.

> TYPICAL SCHEDULE: Team warm-ups—5 min.; agility drills—10 min.; specialties—15 min.; individual drills—20 min.; combination drills—30 min.; team play—40 min. The times listed will vary depending upon the opponent, time of season, and team progress.

Basic drill: Diagram 1 illustrates our basic drill—combination sweep drill right.

1. We'll employ various offensive formations and a variation of defensive sets in our skeleton drills.

2. When the guards and onside end are on offense, the tackles and offside end concentrate on defense.

3. We'll rotate to the combination sweep drill at the end of 15 minutes.

4. Red and Blue offensive skeleton teams rotate in running power sweeps or the variations as illustrated.

> VARIATIONS: Variations to the basic drill are shown in Diagram 2. We have strengthened our power series by including these variations. It helps to keep the defense

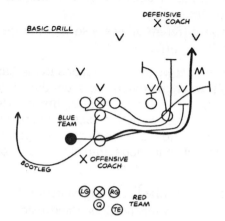

Diagram 1

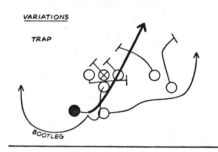

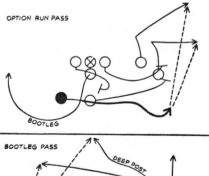

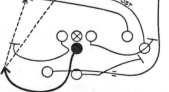

Diagram 2

honest when occasionally the offensive team will run
these variations.

Grey and White teams will run through the identical drills simultaneously. There are times when the drill will call for Blue and Grey teams and Red and White teams to be involved in the workout. Remember, we are emphasizing defense and counter-offense simultaneously.

5

Techniques and Drills for Offensive Center Play

by William D. McHenry

Director of Athletics and Head Football Coach

Washington and Lee University

William D. McHenry is director of athletics, head football coach, and chairman of the Department of Physical Education at Washington and Lee University, Lexington, Virginia. Coach McHenry was formerly with Lebanon Valley (Annville, Pa.) College, Williams (Williamstown, Mass.) College, and Pennsylvania Military Institute, now known as Widener College, in Chester, Pennsylvania.

One of the most under-rated positions on the offensive football team is that of the offensive center. Every play must, of course, start with the center-quarterback exchange—and if any given play is to be successful, it must naturally be initiated with proper timing and execution. There can be no margin for error in the center-quarterback exchange, as the likely exchange will be a fumble.

> NOTE: Too many coaches place a young man at the center position because he is too slow to be a guard, too small to be a tackle, or does not have the coordination and agility to be an end. This is a mistake and can lead to trouble.

Choosing a boy to play the center position requires that a coach examine the many skills and characteristics of his potential lineman. The axiom in baseball about strength down the middle applies equally well in football. A close examination of any successful football team will reveal the same strength down the middle—center, quarterback, and fullback. Here's what we look for in a center and how we coach him.

Characteristics: When you find an athlete with a combination of the following characteristics and traits, you will find a good center candidate: (1) natural athlete with good sense of timing; (2) good hands, ability to handle ball; (3) hard-nosed athlete who can block; (4) sense of concentration; (5) size and quickness; (6) dedication.

> TIP: Even though he's a lineman and should possess all the blocking skills that the other linemen work on, he

must spend a great deal of his practice time with the backs. Too often the backfield coach neglects to work with and make corrections of the center while he's directing the backs. When we're working our offensive team, I personally work with our quarterbacks and centers.

Center-quarterback exchange: There are a great number of ways to teach the exchange. The important thing is to choose a method that will become automatic with your center and quarterback. Adverse playing conditions should have no effect on the method of exchange if it's properly taught. We have long used the straight-arm pendulum swing with the ball turned over on its axis as it's brought directly back into the quarterback's hands. We use it because it's easy to teach a beginner, enables the center to fire out quickly and become a blocker, and because we've had few fumbles with it.

—*Center's stance:* (1) Feet shoulder-width, squared with line of scrimmage; (2) weight forward on balls of feet; (3) ankles and knees bent to form power-producing angles at both joints; (4) head looking straight ahead with neck bulled; (5) hips slightly higher than shoulders; (6) ball should be placed as far out in front of the center as he can reach and still keep his balance; (7) weight evenly distributed between ball and balls of feet.

> NOTE: Lead hand should be placed on the forward point of the ball with the back end of the ball pointing toward the crotch. Angle of the ball must be less than 45°. Forefinger runs down the seam of the ball with the laces turned to the right for a right-handed quarterback (opposite for left-handed quarterback). Guide hand on back portion of ball merely to help with the balance (Diagram 1).

—*Quarterback's stance:* (1) Feet parallel, roughly shoulder width apart; (2) knees bent slightly so that weight is distributed evenly on the feet—weight should be slightly forward and on the inside balls of the feet; (3) hips should be slightly bent in a position where the shoulders are over the knees and squared; (4) head set and looking over defense; (5) elbows slightly bent and tucked in tight to your hips; (6) thumbs overlapped with right thumb on bottom if right-handed (opposite for left-handers); (7) heels of hands pressed together; (8) place knuckles of thumb firmly against the center's buttock with forefingers

Diagram 1

pressed against his leg in a relaxed manner. Be sure fingers are spread and pointing toward the ground.

> EXCHANGE OF BALL: (1) Center steps out with a short jab step as he fires ball firmly into the quarterback's hands with a straight arm pendulum swing; (2) at the point of contact the center's lead hand will be under the ball and the quarterback's hands will close around the ball with the laces across his fingertips; (3) as the center moves forward, the quarterback must maintain pressure with his hands on the center's buttocks by extending his arms until ball is clearly exchanged.

Drill for exchange: After each quarterback and center demonstrates his understanding of the exchange, have all the centers line up on any yard line. Have the quarterbacks step into position—and the coach should give the starting count as he desires. All centers should snap the ball at the precise starting count—and you should hear the exchange at one time. Have the quarterbacks rotate each time so that they work with a different center on each exchange (Diagram 2). Be sure to give the direction of the quarterback and check to see that centers fire out for at least five steps.

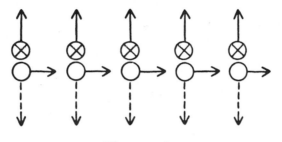

Diagram 2

Deep pass to punter: The importance of the kicking game in football cannot be overemphasized. A blocked punt can be the most demoralizing thing that can happen to a team. Relatively few punts are blocked, however, when the center gets a good snap back to the punter. Pride and confidence must be developed in the center and the punter.

> NOTE: The center's first responsibility is to get the ball back properly to his punter; secondly, he becomes a blocker and must protect the kicker; finally, he must cover the kick with speed and become a tackler.

—*Stance:* This will differ from the stance of his exchange. His weight should be evenly distributed on his feet with good balance. There should be no weight forward on the ball. His legs should be spread a bit wider than his shoulders—with his right foot staggered back toe to heel. Be sure the stance is comfortable and that the center can see the belt buckle of the punter.

—*Grip on ball:* He grips the ball just as if he were throwing a forward pass. He spreads his fingers, grips the laces with the tips of his finger or fingers, and keeps the ball off the palm of his hand. His lead hand should be well forward on the ball depending upon the size of his hands. His guide hand is in the middle or back portion of the ball. His wrists should be cocked and his elbows should be inside his knees.

—Snapping the ball: He should lift the ball slightly off the ground as he whips it through his legs, with good follow-through. He keeps his hands low and aims directly for the belt buckle of his punter. He must get good whip action from his wrists and follow through along the imaginary line to his target. Once the ball has left his hands he should set up in a good blocking position. He should pass the ball with his lead hand; his guide hand is merely helping to keep the ball on target. The ball should be released off his fingertips to get a good spiral action. Emphasize the lifting action at first and this will become automatic.

Drill for snap: Have your centers work in pairs before actually working with your punters. Always have centers start close together at roughly 6 yards, then gradually move back as they develop confidence and accuracy. We ultimately snap at 13-yards' distance (Diagram 3).

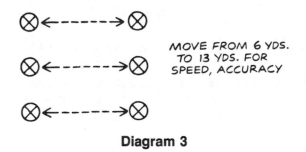

MOVE FROM 6 YDS. TO 13 YDS. FOR SPEED, ACCURACY

Diagram 3

Have your centers snap with their helmets and shoulder pads on. This will make a big difference in their development of the skill. We also like to have someone in front of the center at all times so he realizes the importance of getting set.

> NOTE: There are more techniques that all centers must learn if they are to become an important part of your football team. They must become effective blockers. The blocking skills that are characteristic to all linemen must not be neglected by the centers.

6

Hitting and Blocking Drills

by Chas "Rip" Engle

Former Head Football Coach
Pennsylvania State University

Chas "Rip" Engle's 36-year coaching record is a most impressive one. It began in 1930 at Waynesboro (Pa.) High School, where he posted an 86-18 mark; advanced to Western Maryland College and Brown University; and ended as successfully as it began at Penn State University, where Coach Engle compiled a 104-48 record. Rip Engle, now retired, can boast most deservedly of an overall record of 224-86 and numerous awards—his most cherished being the N.Y.T.D. Club Award in 1967, the Amos Alonzo Stagg Award in 1969, and the National Football Foundation and Hall of Fame 1973.

I make no claim of originality for any of the drills described here. Derived, as they are, from many sources, put together they are a good representation of the best drills used in modern football. All of them, and many others, are used at Penn state; I strongly believe in their value.

The drills described here are used to develop two techniques: (1) Hitting, and (2) one-on-one blocking.

Developing Hitting Technique

In order to properly deliver a blow, especially on defense, it is necessary to develop arm and leg coordination, footwork, and body balance. These drills are used to do this.

Hit Drill (Diagram 1)

Purpose: To develop coordinated movement of the arm and leg when striking a blow from the football position.

Procedure: Both men in semi-crouch, one off-set to the right or left of his opponent. Both men are prepared to crash shoulders. On coach's command of "hit," both step with the same foot and engage with the same shoulder. Players then step back and repeat procedure, usually three times with each shoulder.

Coaching points: Watch to avoid "winding up." Stress simultaneous movement of same arm and leg. Feet must always move. No hitting with the elbow or turning of the body should be allowed.

Diagram 1

Bounce-Shuffle Drill (Diagram 2)

Purpose: Same as that of "Hit" drill.

Procedure: Same as for "Hit" drill only the player represented by the triangle delivers one blow on right then shuffle steps to left and delivers a blow, shuffle steps right, and so on. The movement is repeated until three or four blows have been landed on each shoulder.

Coaching points: Same as "Hit" drill.

Diagram 2

Bounce-Point Reaction (Diagram 3)

Purpose: This is one of our basic "everyday" drills to develop reaction and alertness.

Procedure: Two offensive men line up slightly to the outside of the defender. All three players are in a "hitting" position. The coach stands behind the defender. The drill begins when the coach points to one of the two offensive men. The designated rusher moves in and the defender meets him aggressively. Players then return to starting position and the coach points to either one of them to repeat the drill.

Coaching points: The step by the offensive man must be with his inside shoulder and foot. Defender must react with near foot and shoulder immediately in order to neutralize the shoulder lift. He must not drop step.

Diagram 3

Circle Drill (Diagram 4)

Purpose: To teach proper body balance, footwork, and coordination.

Procedure: It is important that never more than seven men are allowed in the circle and that they are kept at least 2½ yards from the man in the middle. This assures him of having a chance to react. On coach's command "ready," everybody gets in a hitting position. At command "begin," the man in the middle moves his feet up and down and circles to his right or left. The coach should try to teach the men in the perimeter not to charge if the "bull" is looking directly at them. The rushers must come in from the side. They must not come full "blast," but be in enough control of themselves to stop their rush and return to their place in the circle if the middle man turns to take another rusher.

Coaching points: Make sure that the middle man uses both forearms to shed blockers. If blocker is coming from his left, middle man must use left forearm instead of turning to favor his right or stronger forearm.

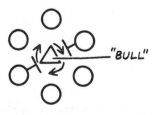

Diagram 4

Somersault-up-Bounce (Diagram 5)

Purpose: To improve reaction and to encourage quick movement of the body.

Procedure: Men line up 5 yards apart in good football position. At command "down," player "A" executes a somersault and quickly comes to his feet in a hitting position. "B" moves forward to meet "A" when "B" is up in hit position. They unload shoulders and forearms while maintaining contact by moving their feet until the command "break" is given.

Coaching points: Players must tuck their heads and cushion fall with hands, arms, and shoulders

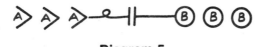

Diagram 5

One-on-One Blocking for Offense

One offensive blocking system requires learning two techniques: (1) The fire-out, or uncoil, and (2) a follow-through maintaining contact. Here are some of the drills we use to coach these techniques:

One-on-One Block (Diagram 6)

Purpose: To develop fundamentals of stance, fire-out, uncoil, and follow-through.

Procedure: Blocker is set on or off the line of scrimmage, first on one shoulder, then on the other of the defensive man. On starting count, blocker unloads on defender and tries to whip him.

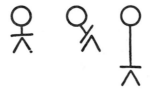

Diagram 6

Coaching points: Good stance—movement on the correct starting count—forehead drive—bringing forearm up to increase blocking surface—head up, tail down—eyes "popped"—short, choppy steps—maintenance of contact as blocker drives.

Belly-Slammer Drill (Diagram 7)

Purpose: To teach shoulder block for controlling a moving object. Also lends conditioning because of "slammer" effect.

Procedure: Two players line up in offensive stance, one in front of each pad of an unweighted Crowther two-man sled. On command "hit," players lunge block and drive the sled back as they land on their stomachs, fully extended on the ground. They then scramble to their feet and regain stance for two more commands of "hit," repeating the procedure quickly each time. After the last "hit," they sprint 10 yards downfield.

Coaching points: The coach should regulate the second and third commands so that the men hit together. He should try to develop the arch of the blockers' backs and stress head up and hips driving forward.

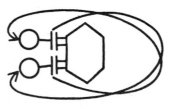

Diagram 7

One-Two Drill (Diagram 8)

Purpose: To teach the coordinated foot action of the shoulder block.

Procedure: Players assume a three-point stance. They fire-out as in the "belly slammer," but do not go to the ground. While firing-out, they bring up the same foot as the blocking shoulder. Blockers must move the sled at least 5 yards.

Coaching points: Players must not "step then hit." The block must be made in a coordinated, *single* movement. They must drive out, not up and follow through while maintaining contact with and driving the sled.

Diagram 8

Push-Pull Drill (Diagram 9)

Purpose: To increase player's ability to maintain contact on turning of an opponent.

Procedure: A single blocker uncoils on one pad of a two-man sled. The coach takes hold of the opposite strut of the sled while the blocker is driving it. The coach can either push or pull the strut, causing the sled to turn. The player must maintain contact with pad.

Coaching points: The coach should not jerk the sled. He should check blocking fundamentals and make especially sure that the blocker keeps his head up. If he doesn't keep his head up, he'll probably fall on his face.

Diagram 9

7

Multiple Trap Blocking Drill

by Ray Cliffe

Head Football Coach

Cleveland (St. Louis, Missouri) High School

Ray Cliffe's record as head football coach at Cleveland High School is 102-65-12 in the tough St. Louis Public High School League (ten teams). His record includes two undefeated teams and a public high school championship.

We use the following multiple drill to save time in teaching our offensive unit team trapping and teaching the interior linebackers to recognize their offensive keys in reading traps and pulling guards.

In Diagram 1, the squares indicate dummy-holders on a five-man line. The two interior linebackers have air dummies and react to the offensive keys.

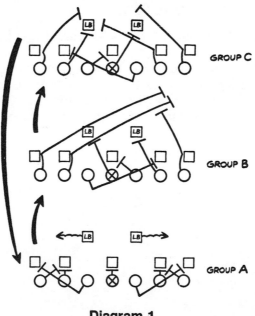

Diagram 1

1. Group A executes "G" blocking (double team trap); the assignment is designed for the outside belly trap. Both guards pull simultaneously to kick out the defensive ends.

2. Group B executes interior "4" hole (pin trap) trap blocking, and Group C executes interior "6" hole (long trap) trap blocking. The defensive linebackers react to the movement of the guards.

The groups rotate, moving from position to position *on the run* at all times; Group C sprints to the Group A position to execute the "G" blocking.

8

Ideas and Drills for Blocking in the Offensive Line

by Harry T. Gamble

Head Football Coach
University of Pennsylvania

Harry T. Gamble became the 17th head football coach at the University of Pennsylvania in November, 1970, succeeding Bob Odell. Gamble returned to the University after having served five years as a Quaker assistant before becoming head coach at Lafayette College for four years. In his last two years at the University of Pennsylvania, Coach Gamble compiled a 12-6 mark, the best at Penn in many years. His 1973 squad finished second in the Ivy League race.

The basic principle of effective line blocking is simplicity; it's nothing more than knowing who and how to block. Who to block is generally determined by a short, concise, and easily applied rule. How to block is the technique used in the application of the rule. It is this second phase of offensive line play that we'll discuss.

> METHODS: There are many different methods by which an offensive lineman can attack an opponent. These vary with the assignments and responsibilities on a given play, and are multiplied considerably by the number of different plays within the various styles of offense in use today.

In deciding what techniques of blocking should be taught, a coach must first analyze his offense to determine what he wants to do—and then teach only those techniques that will best get the job done. In this article, we'll discuss the stance and the techniques and drills of the two basic blocks currently employed by our offensive line in the running game.

Stance

We prefer a four-point stance because it is square (neither right nor left), is balanced (does not have one shoulder lower than the other), and aids in accomplishing a low start for good initial contact. The feet are shoulder-width apart, perpendicular to the line of scrimmage, either foot back in not more than a heel-toe alignment. This will enable movement left, right, and forward. Both of the hands are down under the corresponding shoulder. The fingers are cupped and turned outward in a high arch. The bodyweight should be slightly forward with the back parallel to the ground. The neck is firm but not strained.

> NOTE: Offensive linemen move into their stance by: crisply breaking from the huddle, descending to all fours as they approach the line of scrimmage, and settling in hands first, adjusting the feet later. This avoids delay and the characteristic adjustment by the center, guards, and tackles in that order, and/or a bowed line.

Huddle Drill

Purpose: To develop huddle discipline, tempo, stance, and take-off.

Preliminary position: Hands on knees, facing away from the line of scrimmage, approximately 5 yards behind the line.

Secondary position: Quarterback enters the huddle and says "up." The line immediately comes to attention in an erect stand-up position. Quarterback calls the play once and says "break."

Release: On break, the linemen jump into the air spinning to the inside, landing on both feet facing forward. During the turn, hold the palm of the inside hand up in front of the inside hip, elbow close to the body. The outside hand and arm are swung up and over in a high arc and brought down with a resounding clap on the stationary hand. Race to the line of scrimmage, lowering into position on the way. Set the hands first, then adjust the feet. Get set quickly. We do this five or six times daily.

Reach Block

Target: Aim for the outside portion of the opponent's far knee. (Defender in the blocker's *on gap*.)

Approach: The initial step should be short and controlled, made with the near foot.

Point of contact: The forehead portion of the helmet and nose guard should be driven through the opponent's leg. If this is executed properly, the blocker's head will end up outside of the defender's knee.

CAUTION: The blocker must drive his head into the opponent. Overreaching will result in poor contact initially and loss of opponent.

Follow-through: At contact, the hips of the blocker should be swung in such a manner that the blocker's body is pointed straight upfield. If this hip swing is done too soon, the blocker can be overpowered. The defender must first be neutralized by the head being driven through his legs. Sustain contact until the whistle blows. If the defender attempts to back away and pursue, the blocker should fight to a two-point blocking position and keep after him. If the inside shoulder should dip, the blocker should jam his outside hand to the ground to square his shoulders and scramble on all fours.

NOTE: For the reach block (defender *on* the blocker), the target is adjusted to the inside to avoid overreaching; i.e., inside of the opponent's knee, crotch, etc., so long as the blocker's head gets through the defender's leg to the outside. Likewise, the angle of attack will also be reduced. The remainder of the block remains essentially the same.

Drills: In a controlled daily drill in which a defender catches the blocker's head, the target, approach, point of contact and follow-through are all taught, emphasized, and reviewed.

Make the offensive man sustain his block for 15 to 20 yards downfield. Insist that the defender work against the blocker's head. Emphasize second effort by throwing the ball an additional 10 to 15 yards downfield, making both the blocker and defender sprint to it to end the drill. During the drill, the coach should stay as close to the blocker and defender as possible, yelling critical comments. Insist on proper technique. Stop and start again if necessary (Diagram 1).

The hip swing can be emphasized on the seven-man crowther sled by lining up seven blockers, one man to the left of the machine (Diagram 2). At the signal, they reach block to the pad to their right with the emphasis on proper hip swing at contact. The procedure is reversed to the left.

Once the rudiments of the block are mastered, at least once or twice a week, live one-on-one reach blocking can be carried on in a regular drill period (Diagram 3).

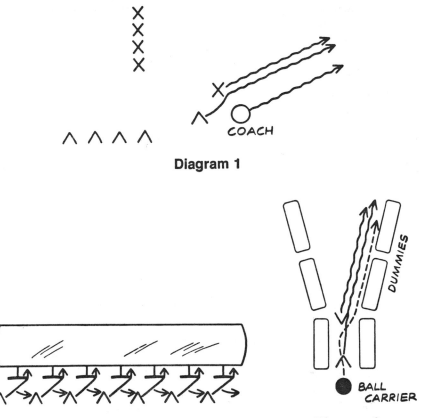

Diagram 1

Diagram 2   **Diagram 3**

Fire-Out Block

Target: There is no special target except the middle of the defender. Contact should be only high enough so that a free hand of the blocker could touch the ground.

Approach: Drive off the line of scrimmage as quickly as possible maintaining a head-up, flat-back position. Maximum impact upon contact is necessary to neutralize the defensive man's charge. The first step is short and controlled. If the defender is gapped, step with the near foot. If he is *on*, step with the rear foot. After the first step, maintain a wide base and carry out short control steps.

Contact: The point of contact is the forehead portion of the blocker's helmet. Fight to keep the head up. Such action will aid in maintaining balance and sustaining the block. Keep the head up, back arched, and knees flexed.

Follow-through: Maintain a wide base and carry out short control steps. Balance and control is a must. To facilitate good balance, the arms should be moved as in normal running action.

> COACHING POINTS: Develop a quick, explosive start; keep eyes open and on the target; once contact has been made, the feet never stop; keep head up, back flat, feet spread, and knees flexed; never allow knees to touch the ground.

Drills

Fire-out #1: The purpose is to emphasize the forehead as point of contact, bulled neck, and head-up position.

Break position: A defender behind and holding a large blocking bag; a blocker in a four-point stance, forehead and nose guard nuzzled up in contact with the bag.

Go: The blocker drives the dummy 5 yards with short, driving steps, pumping arms in running fashion. Only contact is with the forehead and nose guard.

Fire-out #2: The purpose is to teach the complete fire-out block.

Break position: A blocker in a four-point stance 2 yards away from a dummy. A defender behind and holding a large blocking bag.

Go: Fire out aggressively making initial contact with forehead and nose guard, driving dummy 5 yards.

> COACHING POINTS: Maintain a flat back, good base, short, driving steps, and head-up position. Good arm action will aid follow-through at impact.

9

Primary Line Blocking and Drills to Perfect It

by John T. Federici

Head Football Coach

Nutley (New Jersey) High School

John T. Federici has been coaching high school football for 15 years. As head football coach at Passaic (N.J.) High School, he compiled a record of 67-30-2, which included two state championships and two conference championships. Since 1971 he has been head football coach at Nutley (N.J.) High School. His overall mark is 96-44-4.

We adhere to the fact that blocking and tackling are still the prime ingredients of successful football. Thus, if we can block and tackle just a little better than our opponents, we'll win.

> NOTE: Our offense constitutes fast-hitting, straight-ahead plays, power plays, and passes from both play action and drop-back action.

Therefore, our stance must be one which will enable us to perform all aspects of the line play required in these offenses. Our linemen must be able to move forward, laterally and backward without any change in original position. Here's how we teach stance and blocking to get what we want done.

Stance: In teaching stance, we work in two units—guards and centers in one and tackles and ends in the other. Basically, all stances are the same because all the linemen have pulling assignments. We put our linemen in an upright position, feet pointed straight ahead, parallel and shoulder-width apart; the toe to instep set depends upon the height of the individual. We next go to a sitting position with the bodyweight placed on the balls of the feet and the knees directly over the ankles.

> TIP: The back should be straight, with the hips slightly higher than the shoulders so as to fire out or pull without having to first lift the tail. The head is up, neck slightly bulled, and eyes looking through the blocking target.

The down hand is now placed on the ground just inside the back knee, bridged either on the first row of knuckles or fingertips. This hand is primarily for balance and should not throw the shoulders out of line. The arm not used in the tripod is placed across the thigh, forearm parallel to the ground, fist loosely clenched and ready to be used if necessary. If positioned correctly, the stance will be squared.

> COACHING POINT: It's imperative that the lineman learn to control his weight in the stance. The down hand should be able to be taken away without the lineman losing complete body balance. With such control, he should be able to move in any direction without loss of speed, power, and drive.

Chute drill: We have one teaching aid which we use daily—our stance and start chute drill (Diagram 1). Most high school boys have a tendency to relax—and if not checked daily, they will lose the effectiveness of the proper stance. It is with this thought in mind that we practice stance and start each day throughout the season.

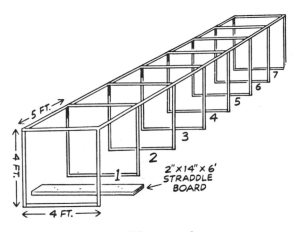

Diagram 1

> PROCEDURE: By placing a straddle board in each stall, we force the lineman to keep a wide base. The chute forces him to stay low and in a football position. As the individual goes through, we check proper body alignment, stance, head-and-back position, fire-out speed, and chugging procedure. By placing a dummy at the end of the straddle board, we can check for proper contact—hit, lift, and drive procedure.

Drive block: In teaching the drive block, we emphasize fire-out—correct extension and getting to the defensive man before he crosses the neutral zone. We check stance to make sure the offensive lineman is coiled properly so as to explode on the count. The forehead is aimed directly at the middle of the defensive man's body. At full extension, the head comes up, eyes looking for treetops—keeping the neck bulled and on contact with the forehead, we begin our lift and drive.

One-on-one drill: The drill we use to help teach drive blocking is shown in Diagram 2. The personnel involved include the offensive line, center, quarterback, and coach.

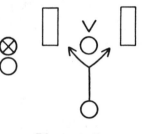

Diagram 2

PROCEDURE: Place the defensive man between two dummies about 3 yards apart. Put an offensive blocker over him with a ball carrier 3 yards behind. On the count, the blocker will drive block the defensive man, and the ball carrier will run for daylight. We check proper stance, fire-out on count, contact position, and drive.

Straight shoulder block: We use the straight shoulder block when the defense is head up and must be moved in a definite direction to open the running lane, or when he's an aggressive defender. The basic principles of the drive block are not altered—except that just before making contact, the head is slid past the opponent's hips to the proper side. The blocker hits with his shoulder and upper arm bent at the elbow, parallel to the ground. On contact, the foot corresponding with the contact shoulder should be so placed that it is in the center of the defensive man's stance; the other foot is on the outside and working to a position beyond the defensive man.

NOTE: By so doing a wide base is created, with the feet chugging and gaining ground. Shoulders should be squared and the drive should be directly through the defender and not around him, so as not to have the feet blocking the running lane.

Angle block: When we are drive blocking and movement is attained by the offensive man, the instant he begins to feel the defensive man choose his route, he then goes into an angle block to ride him out. It is also used when the defensive man is either inside or outside our blocker. We step toward the defensive man with the near foot, contact is made above the hips with the desired shoulder and forearm—and with chugging feet we work in closer to the opponent, gaining desired lift and movement down the line.

Angle block drill: A drill we use to develop angle blocking technique is shown in Diagram 3. The drill includes the offensive linemen, defensive linemen, and the coach.

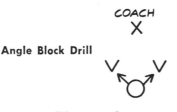

Diagram 3

PROCEDURE: Place one offensive lineman and two defensive men as shown in Diagram 3. On the count, both defensive men charge straight ahead; the offensive man blocks the defensive man indicated by the coach. We check for proper step, contact, and drive.

Pulling to trap: In trapping, we use two basic trap blocks—the long and short; techniques for the two are identical. On the count, the trapping lineman steps laterally with the foot nearest the direction of the pull. His second step with his far foot (pivot foot) should be down the line towards his opponent. The trapper, by taking short, driving steps and hugging the line of scrimmage, will be under control and capable of exploding into any defensive man who may penetrate the neutral zone—even though he may not be his assigned block. On contact, the foot corresponding with the contact should be placed in the center of the defensive man's stance, while the head is placed to the downfield side.

Trapping drills: Our trapping drills, as shown in Diagrams 4 and 5, help teach the proper techniques of trapping various types of charging linemen.

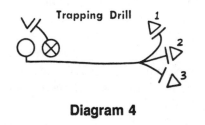

Diagram 4

POWER TRAP   INFLUENCE TRAP

BOARD TRAP DR.

Diagram 5

PROCEDURE: Place an offensive center and guard as shown in Diagram 4. Over the guard, place a defensive man in the trapping zone, place three defensive men holding air dummies. In position 1, the trapper will use an over block in an attempt to seal the defender to the inside. In position 2, the defender is waiting in the hole and the trapper must drive him down the line. In position 3, the defender has penetrated beyond the line and the trapper needs only to screen him by staying between the defender and the ball carrier.

On the count, the trapper will begin his pull. On his second step, the coach calls a number to indicate which defender the trapper will block. We check for proper stance, steps, contact, and drive of the trapper—and also for proper fill by the center for the pulling guard. Diagram 5 shows our board trap drill that we use with the same objectives in mind.

Pass protection: We utilize two basic types of pass plays—passes which develop after the fake of a run and straight drop-back passes. Our basic plan for drop-back protection is to form a cup, with the center and interior linemen as the inside of the cup and the backs not in the pattern at the cup's edges. Each lineman is responsible for a designated area to protect. The center protects directly in front, the width of his shoulders; guards protect from inside gap to outside shoulder; tackles protect from inside gap to outside shoulder.

> BLOCKING ZONE: The backs are responsible for the outer edges of the cup, the area between the tackles and themselves. Linemen are coached to remain inside the blocking area and to read their blocks from the inside out. Our blocking zone is shown in Diagram 6.

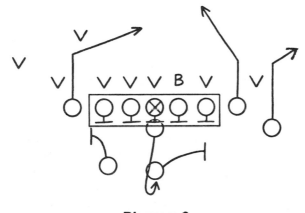

Diagram 6

The depth of the blocking zone is determined by the line of scrimmage as the forward edge and by the linemen's retreat as the rear edge. The maximum retreat for the linemen is 3 yards. By remaining in this zone, he should cause no interference with the passer's moves nor with his vision.

The major cause of cup breakdown is permitting the defensive man to make contact with the offensive blockers before they are set. To offset this, we fire out on the defensive man, make contact, then retreat, and set up in the set position. This is tail down, knees bent, feet chugging, with head up, eyes on the target, and the body set to deliver a blow.

> NOTE: After contact has been made and the charge of the rusher has been neutralized, we step back slightly into a set position ready to strike again. From the set position, we aim the forehead at the numbers, continually protecting the inside.

Pass blocking drill: This drill shown in Diagram 7 helps to teach the techniques of drop-back pass protection. We use both the offensive and defensive line and the coach.

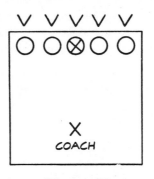

Diagram 7

> PROCEDURE: Have offensive linemen and defensive linemen lined up opposite each other at the front of the square. The coach stands 7 yards deep. On the count, the offensive linemen protect the passer for 4 seconds (we try to have the ball delivered within 3 seconds, thereby giving us more of a controlled game and less breakdown). We check for stance, fire-out, and steps for proper set position. We also work on overloads; respecting fakes; and blocking the three possible rushes: inside, outside, and over the man.

10

Drills for Developing Pass Receivers

by Robert A. Martin

Assistant Football Coach

Westfield (New Jersey) High School

Robert A. Martin is assistant football coach under head coach Gary Kehler at Westfield (N.J.) High School. Coach Martin's "B" squad can boast of 102 straight victories. The varsity squad, under Coach Kehler, has had 33 straight victories, three unbeaten seasons; he has also compiled eight conference titles, four state sectional titles, and two state championships.

At Westfield High School, we feel that pass receiving is an important phase of our football offense. Although we stress a ball-control offense, the passing game has enabled us to loosen up many a defense.

> NOTE: Our basic offensive set is an unbalanced line with a slot to the short side and a wing to the long side (Diagram 1). From this set, we have the option of employing four quick receivers. Therefore, it is essential to our offensive thinking that we develop good receivers.

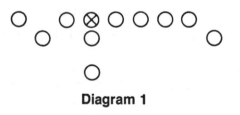

Diagram 1

Types of Releases

The release off the line is important to the success of running a good pattern. It is important because most defenses try to hold up receivers on the line to:

1. Destroy the timing between receiver and quarterback;
2. Help in the pass rush.

Therefore, we must drill to perfect more than one type of release. The first release that we drill on is—dip a shoulder, windmill that arm, and step out with the opposite foot.

The second release is—drive directly into the man and roll either way to clear the line. The third release is—scramble on all fours with head up. There are, of course, many other releases, but these are the basic ones that we utilize.

> NOTE: Another point is—our receivers talk to each other after the huddle is broken or at the line of scrimmage, about the type of release they will take.

Pass Routes and Alignment

The next step in pass receiving is the proper route and alignment. The drills we use here are simple but most effective. We place receivers in two lines and place a scrimmage vest at 7 yards. Our thinking is that at 7 yards we will make our pass cuts, and if there is one set mark that our cuts are made at, it will help the timing between quarterback and receiver.

The only exception for adjustment of this mark is down and distance or field position. From these two lines we run all our routes both left and right with the 7-yard mark. During the drill, we put a stopwatch on the receivers to check their speed. Once the receivers have the mark timed, the scrimmage vest is removed and the patterns run. This mark and time will be checked throughout practice to keep it constant.

> NOTE: After the routes are learned, then the receivers can put the three skills of releasing and the pattern together. From here we progress to the down and distance situation: 3rd and 7, 4th and 5, etc., and field position: running a square-out into the short line and also how to adjust an alignment when at a wide-out position.

Drill Program

Once the release and routes are drilled, then the most important phase is concentration on the ball and catching it. Here are a few drills we use to perfect these techniques.

One-handed catch: The one-handed catch is illustrated in Diagram 2. We line up the receivers and run them down about 5 yards, and then toss the ball to the right and the left of the receivers. With eyes on the ball, the receiver one-hands it and pulls the ball into his body.

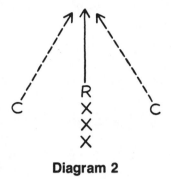

Diagram 2

Sideline catch: The sideline catch is a difficult one because most receivers either take their eyes off the ball or catch the ball out-of-bounds. We try drilling to make this a common catch.

The coach throws the ball (Diagram 3) so that the receiver makes the catch and keeps 2 feet in-bounds. The throws are easy at first so that the boys can catch them—then their difficulty is increased.

> NOTE: The rule in high schools is only 1 foot in-bounds, but we drill 2 feet in-bounds just to be safe and to give the receiver confidence.

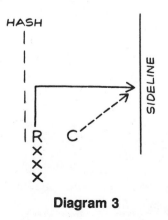

Diagram 3

High-low drill: The receivers line up across the field with their backs toward the coach (Diagram 4). On a given signal they turn, ready to receive the ball. The ball is thrown to one receiver, high or low, left or right.

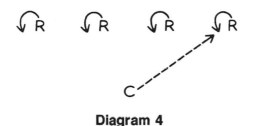

Diagram 4

NOTE: This drill trains the receiver not catching the ball to be ready and to look for it. Another point is that in prepractice two receivers can get together and work on their own.

Tip drill: For our tip drill (Diagram 5) we have the receivers run a route—square-out, hook, post—and then in the area where the reception will take place, we have a manager stand and tip the ball. The receiver must react to the tipped ball and make the catch.

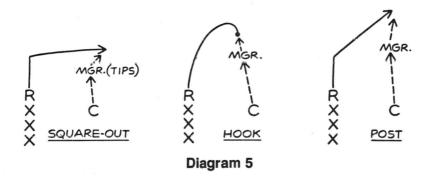

Diagram 5

Run-the-lines drill: Here we place two receivers on yard lines, 10 yards apart. On a given signal the two run the lines, looking over their inside shoulder. The coach throws the ball down the middle and the two receivers go for the ball.

NOTE: The one catching the ball tries to score at the opposite sideline; the receiver who loses the fight for the ball tries to prevent it.

Other factors: There are many more drills but these are the basic ones that we use. Other factors that are important for pass receivers are—catching the ball while facing the sun; making a catch in the end zone; and adjustment to different types of coverages.

Running with the Ball

The last phase in receiving is running with the ball after catching it. Some of the drills we use in this respect are as follows:

1. Have the receiver catch the ball, head-fake one way, and dip the shoulder and go opposite.

2. Hit the man after he makes the catch with an air bag.

3. We are fortunate in having a "Smitty Blaster"—we catch the ball and go through the blaster.

Conclusion

After practicing all these phases, we put them together and work combination pass routes with and without a defense. Once a week we practice our 2-minute offense, which has paid off for us greatly during the season. This is basically how we train our receivers at Westfield High School—and it has proven rewarding for us.

11

Ideas and Drills for Running the Cut and Catching the Ball

by Marty Pierson

Former Assistant Football Coach

Duke University

Marty Pierson has been retired from football coaching since 1971. He last served as an assistant football coach at Duke University under head coach Mike McGee.

At Duke University, we began experimenting with the swing-end formation (Diagram 1) in 1955 and ran it periodically through the 1959 season. Before the 1960 season, we decided to specialize in this type offense and since then have run virtually nothing else.

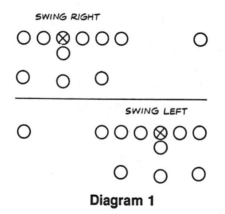

Diagram 1

SIDELINE CUT: Our best pattern from this formation has been the sideline cut. Since 1960, we have completed 271 of 400 sideline passes attempted for a .678 percentage.

The 271 passes completed gained 2,479 yards. Only five of these passes have been intercepted. Two of the interceptions occurred when the pass was thrown to the halfback, and the other three resulted from busted patterns when the quarterback threw the ball after scrambling. This means that of the 400 passes—not a single pass thrown to the swing-end under normal conditions had been intercepted.

Running sequence: Diagram 2 shows the running sequence the receiver must follow to run a satisfactory sideline cut. We break down the sequence as follows: *Sprint*—The receiver sprints off the line of scrimmage to beat the defensive man playing him. *Let up*—As the receiver gets speed, he must let up with his weight leaning backward to get ready to stop. *Stop, cut, sprint out*—The steps of the sideline cut are similar to those of the "column right" maneuver in military marching.

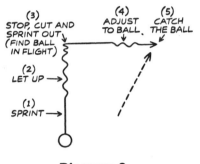

Diagram 2

DIAGRAM 3: When the receiver is making a right sideline cut, he must stop his forward motion on his right foot, then plant his left foot directly in front of the right at about a 45-degree angle. The receiver now makes the cut and is in the position to sprint out. When you cut to the right, the forward motion must be completely stopped as the right foot hits the ground. The cut should be exactly 90 degrees—and if it's not square, it will be more difficult for the receiver to quickly find the ball in flight.

Sprint-out thrust: The left leg supplies the thrust for the sprint-out of the "column right" maneuver. At this point, there are three distinctly different movements: (1) Stop the forward motion; (2) make a 90-degree cut; (3) supply the thrust for the sprint-out in the new direction. It is physically impossible to make all three movements in

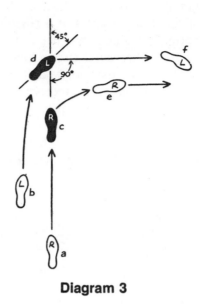

Diagram 3

one motion—you must have stopped your forward motion·when the right foot hits the ground, and then make your cut and supply the thrust from the left foot.

Foot position: When the receiver's feet are in positions (a), (b), and (c) in Diagram 3, an imaginary line drawn through his hips would be parallel to the line of scrimmage. When his left foot is in position (d), his hips begin to turn, and as the right foot lands in position (e), the hips have turned 90 degrees. As the left foot reaches position (f), the hips have turned an additional 90 degrees.

> NOTE: This means that the body and the hips turn 180 degrees, allowing the receiver to have his back to the defender. The receiver must simultaneously sprint out and whip his head around to find the ball in flight.

Adjust to the ball: After finding the ball in flight, the receiver must adjust to it, get his body in proper position, and catch the ball. Diagram 4 shows our position techniques for adjusting to the ball in flight and minimizing the possibilities of an interception.

(a) If the pass is thrown perfectly, the receiver should sprint about four steps out of the cut and catch the ball running at full speed.

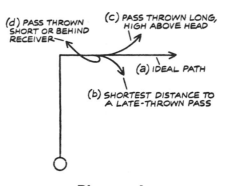

Diagram 4

(b) If the pass is thrown short, he must come back toward the line of scrimmage and catch the ball so that his body is between the ball and the defender.

(c) If the pass is thrown long, and high above the head of the receiver, he must adjust his depth downfield and catch the ball high.

> NOTE: Our reason for insisting on an exact 90-degree cut and *not* coming back toward the line of scrimmage is that you increase the possibility of an interception when you come back.

(d) If the pass is thrown short and behind the receiver, he must make a complete turn and come back to the ball—and if at all possible, catch the ball with his body between the ball and the defender.

Bad pass drill: The primary purpose of this drill is to teach the receiver to come back to a pass thrown behind him. The receivers are lined up to the coach's right as shown in Diagram 5. The coach is the passer. The receiver runs 5 yards downfield and comes across laterally, with his hips in a position so that the imaginary line drawn through them is parallel to the line of scrimmage. He is facing the coach, who throws the ball shoulder high behind the receiver so that he cannot catch it by reaching back—but must change his running direction by taking short, choppy steps and run back in the opposite direction. After running the drill in this fashion, it is repeated with the receivers approaching from the left.

> COACHING POINTS: An imaginary line drawn through the receiver's hips should be parallel to the line of

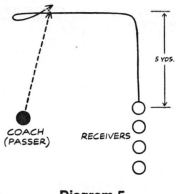

Diagram 5

scrimmage—and he should run with the feet in a cross-step motion so that he can adjust to the ball.

Net drill: We use the "net drill" as shown in Diagram 6 to teach finding the ball in the air. The receiver stands about 2 yards from the

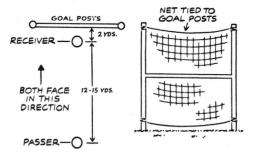

Diagram 6

net and facing it; the passer also faces the net about 12 to 15 yards from the receiver. On the command "turn," the receiver must whip his head around, turn his body to the right or left (predetermined by the coach), find the ball, and catch it. We time it out so that the ball is very near the receiver when he turns around—so he has just enough time to find the ball, get his hands in the proper position, and catch it. It is advisable to throw the ball so that it is caught chest high or above.

EYES ON THE BALL: The second principle of catching a football is to keep your eyes on the ball. Once the receiver has found the ball in flight, he must give his complete concentration to the ball and have his eyes glued to it until it is caught and put away. Probably the most common error in pass receiving is trying to run with the ball before it is caught.

12

Drills for Developing Concentration in Pass Receiving

by Hugh "Duffy" Daugherty

Former Head Football Coach

Michigan State University

Hugh "Duffy" Daugherty, one of the most successful and famous of modern-day athletic personalities, retired as head football coach at Michigan State in 1972. He left behind one of the most impressive records in the game—105-61-4—and numerous Big Ten titles and Bowl victories.

Perhaps the greatest single factor in catching a football is "concentration." We have all seen many fine ends drop the easy pass, and the same receiver turn right around and catch the tough one—because it was tough and because he did make the great effort.

> IT CAN BE DONE: At Michigan State, we feel that any boy who will teach himself to concentrate can become a good receiver. Some will become better than others because of a touch for the ball—but most can learn to catch the ball well if they will drill to develop concentration.

Here's a series of drills we use with our receivers to help develop concentration. They do the job for us.

Game of catch: The first is a simple game of catch. Two men stand about 6 to 8 feet apart and toss the ball with a soft, two-handed toss back and forth. No effort is made to make the toss an accurate one, but rather to direct the ball in a scattered pattern. As the receiver catches the ball, he must put both hands and eyes on it. The phrase "two eyes and two hands" is the watchword. We make certain that the head and eyes follow the ball until it is tossed back.

Bull pen: The passer (coach or quarterback) stands about 10 yards from the receiver and passes to the receiver who is facing him. Once again, "two eyes and two hands" is the call. The first few passes will be soft and easy to catch. Then the tone of the pass is increased and the pattern is scattered to make the receiver work hard on moving for the ball, while trying to get *both* hands on it.

NOTE: Increase the pace of the ball from day to day until the receiver can handle a ball thrown much harder than your passer would ever deliver in a game.

Over the shoulder: This drill is similar to the "bull pen" except that the receiver has his back turned and takes the ball over the shoulder—first right and then left, finishing with the ball being lobbed directly over the top.

Advanced drill: This drill is more advanced and should be used only after the receiver is having success with the others. On this one, the passer stands about 20 yards from the receiver, who has his back toward the passer. The receiver is instructed to make a quick turn (first to his right) on the signal "turn." As the ball leaves the passer's hand, the passer gives the signal "turn" and the receiver reacts, finds the ball, and catches it.

PRACTICE: A little practice by the passer will enable him to time the throw so that the ball gets there just as the receiver is turning. The pace of the ball is at first soft, but is increased as the drill progresses. After the receiver has made several catches turning to his right, he then changes to his left. The passer should always throw the ball to the side the receiver is turning.

Pressure drill: Diagram 1 illustrates our drill that emphasizes catching the ball under pressure. The receiver lines up in a straight line

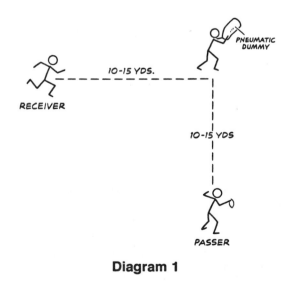

Diagram 1

about 20 yards from the passer—and far enough to his left so that a 15- to 20-yard run will bring him directly in front of the pressure man. The pressure man is one of your receivers holding a pneumatic dummy by the end so that he can swing it into the receiver.

On the command "go," the receiver runs along the line toward the pressure man. The coach or passer is instructed to pass the ball to the receiver just before he gets to the pressure man. As the receiver gets in front of the pressure man, the pneumatic dummy is brought down through the ball and arms.

> THREE POSITIONS: We stress throwing to three positions—(1) throw so that the catch is made before impact of the dummy; (2) throw so that the ball and the dummy are there at the same time; (3) throw so that the impact is made before the catch.

This is probably the finest teaching aid I know to make a boy keep his eyes open and concentrate under pressure. You will notice an almost immediate improvement between the first and second time through this drill. When all your receivers have run from left to right through the drill, turn them around and run them through the other way.

Remember these tips for improving pass receiving:

● A boy must be sold on keeping both eyes and both hands on the ball.

● An effort to get both hands on the ball will make the receiver move his whole body to the ball, not just one arm.

● Concentration with both eyes will keep your receiver after the bobbled, or batted, ball, and will enable him to come up with the catch before it hits the ground.

● Watch your receiver's head. It should snap toward the hands just as the ball does.

● Practice under pressure to learn to catch under pressure.

● Proper handling of the ball after the catch should also be stressed during drills—the ball must be put away and both ends covered after the catch to avoid fumbles on contact.

● Concentration becomes habit with constant drill.

13

Scramble Drill for Drop-Back Passing

by Pete Dyer

Head Football Coach
Pearl River (New York) High School

Pete Dyer is a veteran of some 24 years of coaching—during which time he has accumulated a 121-65-5 record. A noted coach's coach, he is a featured speaker at some of the top football clinics in the nation and the author of over 40 football articles published in leading national magazines, as well as the 1967 volume, *The Flip-Flop Offense in High School Football*, and his most recent book, *Coaching the Wishbone-T Triple Option Attack*. Lately, Coach Dyer has been successfully coaching the Wishbone-T Triple Option—and taking Pearl River to its most successful league season in the past 15 years.

The high school passer must be drilled daily on all the pass patterns that you use. He must throw accurately or all is lost. Thus, it's essential that he drill a great deal on his accuracy by throwing at tires, archery targets, and the like.

> SCRAMBLE DRILL: To help perfect accuracy for drop-back passing, try the scramble drill (Diagram 1). It's a simple drill and thus a time-saver.

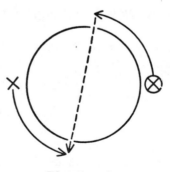

Diagram 1

Execution: Two quarterbacks pair up on a chalk-lined circle (20 to 30 yards apart) directly opposite one another, with one boy holding a football in readiness to throw to his partner across the circle.

MECHANICAL AND SAFETY FEATURE: Since an essential mechanical and safety feature in the drop-back
action is the technique of holding the ball high with both
hands during the entire retreat to the throwing position,
stress employing this technique during the drill.

At a signal from the coach, the boys begin to run to their right
around the circle. While doing so, they play catch with one another,
throwing and catching on the run.

If both boys are right-handed and moving to their right, they will
be throwing *with the grain*, or with their body motion. When the two
quarterbacks reverse the procedure and go in the opposite direction, or
to their left, they will be running and throwing *against the grain*, or
against their body motion.

VALUE: The value of the scramble drill is that it
teaches the drop-back passing quarterback to throw
off-balance and on the dead run, both with and against
the grain. This may very well be necessary on any
drop-back passing play when the pass-protection
blocking breaks down.

14

Quarterback Passing Fundamentals: Techniques and Drills

by Joseph Lauletta

Associate Professor, Physical Education

Tufts (Medford, Massachusetts) University

Joseph Lauletta has been coaching high school and college football since 1957. He was head coach at Northeast Catholic (Philadelphia, Pa.) High School for four years; backfield coach at Wesleyan (Middletown, Conn.) University for two years. At present, he is backfield coach and associate professor in physical education at Tufts University.

Although repetitious passing drills can never guarantee the development of the outstanding quarterback, they are of proven importance in helping the passer achieve his primary objective—completing the forward pass.

> NOTE: Finger control, foot movement, balance, delivery, and reaction time must be considered when developing the mechanics and techniques of the passer. We design our drills with these factors in mind so that they are always meaningful and with purpose.

The fingers (Diagram 1), not the palm, control the football. The sensitive pads of the fingertips actually grip the ball with the palm raised off the surface. The grip should be firm but not so hard as to fatigue the forearm muscles.

Ball Control Drills

In order to stress finger control over the football, we use a series of ball control drills. All movements are done in a firm, positive, but relaxed fashion.

1. *Grip, release, regrip.* Assume correct, comfortable passing grip. Release ball, while pulling it back to hand, and regrip without using the other hand. This is done with the ball in various positions as it moves from center exchange point to passing height.

2. *Finger flip, catch.* Holding the ball palm up with the fingers

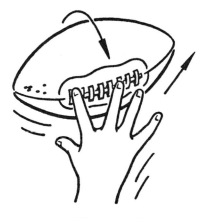

Diagram 1

(ball can be held wth laces running either parallel or perpendicular to the middle—Diagram 1), flip the ball up with fingers and wrist. Attempt to control the number of revolutions and catch it with original grip. Flip the ball so that it rotates away from the hand.

3. *Circus.* Maintain complete control of ball through various movements (hand to hand and toss) behind back, under leg, bounce, spinning on palm, etc.

The above series can be done while standing still or running through a designated route. These ball control drills are installed to better familiarize the quarterback with the handling of the ball in a great variety of circumstances.

> NOTE: Throwing the ball while being hit, the poor snap, the missed hand-off—these and any number of events occur and force the quarterback to regain control of the ball rapidly but confidently.

While some young quarterbacks possess a natural passing arm, many others must work extremely hard to develop the ability to throw well. But all, finally, release the ball in a similar manner. Detailed studies of ball delivery show that the fingers release the ball successively from the little finger to the index finger (Diagram 1). This insures a natural follow-through with the palm down and wrist rotation away from the body. A tight, true spin with many revolutions is the result of a good delivery.

Tufts Dart Drill

Our Tufts dart drill is used for progressively teaching finger control, ball release, and delivery, with balance and follow-through.

Phase one: Two passers stand sidewise facing opposite directions, about 8 yards apart. They hold the ball high, with feet and shoulders stationary, and *dart* the ball to each other (Diagram 2A). Concentrate on correct finger release and arm follow-through, getting maximum spin on ball while keeping it high.

Phase two: From the same position add the shoulder turn and *dart* the ball (Diagram 2B). Leverage is now felt, but you should continue to concentrate on finger control, arm follow-through, and keeping the ball high.

Phase three: Incorporate the rhythm of the left hand in helping turn the body and point the left hand toward the receiver prior to release (Diagram 2C). Develop a smooth, fluid delivery. (The feet have remained stationary through all of the first three phases.)

Phase four: Coordinate placing ball above head, turning the shoulders with the help of the left hand, and stepping with the left foot, simultaneously (Diagram 2D). At this point, the passer can begin to add weight transfer from right to left foot, coordinating it with the release of the ball.

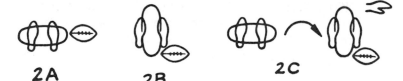

Feet · Shoulders · Ball · Hand · Turn — Legend

2A   2B   2C

2D

Diagram 2

NOTE: The dart drill in its four phases attempts to break down the critical elements of the pass, and, in doing so, points out the importance of every vital phase. Correct application will ultimately result in a complete, fluid, natural motion.

Pass Pattern

During our pass pattern introduction period, we stress consistency of patterns. This is true of both prime and control receivers. Chalkboard patterns, we find, must be walked through and explained on the field with a dummy defense in order to expect full understanding of the receiver's course and probable defensive reaction.

Pass Progression Drill

For illustrative purposes, we'll use the familiar out-pattern with sprint-out set technique. This drill is broken down into three phases.

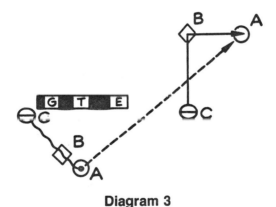

Diagram 3

1. Position—pass catch—0 position (Diagram 3A): The quarterback sets 6-yards deep behind tackle; the receiver sets in the expected reception position. Quarterback passes ball to receiver, concentrating on accuracy while using finger control, hip rotation, transfer of weight from back to front foot, and complete follow-through.

2. Break—pass catch— position (Diagram 3B): The quarterback holds the ball chest high, two steps away from set position. On

command, he continues back to the set position. The receiver positions himself at his pattern breaking point. On same command he breaks and completes the pattern. The quarterback now works on his foot action and balance in relation to a moving target—in addition to releasing the ball.

   3. Line of scrimmage—pass catch—   position (Diagram 3C): In this phase, the quarterback and receiver go through the complete pass-action play. The quarterback sprints out from the line of scrimmage to his set position with ball chest high, looking in passing area.

> TIP: We teach stepping out before snap count in order to facilitate getting to position as quickly as possible.

The receiver releases from the line of scrimmage and runs through his full pattern, catching the ball at the predetermined target position.

> NOTE: We have found that by designing a progressing course in the teaching of passing fundamentals, we are able to dissect, and then hopefully correct, any flaws in the passer's delivery.

15

Selecting and Developing an Offensive Quarterback

by Walt Beaulieu

Former Head Football Coach

Portsmouth (New Hampshire) High School

Walter Beaulieu retired from coaching in 1970. Previously, he was head football coach at Foxcroft (Dover-Foxcroft, Me.) Academy for six years and head football coach at Portsmouth High School for two years.

The total success of our offensive game is dependent upon our quarterback's ability to direct our running game. However, he must be capable of throwing enough passes to complement the running game. We firmly believe that if our quarterback has both speed and agility, he can develop into a proficient passer through hard work and constant practice.

> DRILL PROGRAM: We continually search for drills that will help our quarterback mature into a capable passer and instill confidence in his ability to score with the passing game when needed. Here are some drills that have been effective for our type of offensive game.

Spring practice drills: The first set of drills is used in our spring sessions and stresses techniques that concentrate on the mechanics of passing and correct body movement.

1. Throwing from one knee. The purpose here is to emphasize the importance of wrist snap. Kneel on one knee, knee down on side of passing arm. The wrist snap must be used because from this position it's impossible to get the whole body into the throw. Be careful to avoid the tendency of winding up; make sure the boy keeps the nose of the ball up.

2. Follow-through. Here we over-emphasize the follow-through until the correct form is mastered. The quarterback draws the ball back with both hands just outside his right ear. As the ball is thrown, the passer continues all the way through until his hand reaches the opposite hip. The feet should be parallel to each other at the end of the throw.

NOTE: Have the receiver start at 5 yards; then increase the distance. The receiver should place his hands in different positions to give the quarterback various targets.

3. Stance and footwork. Have the quarterback assume his stance by taking a natural step forward and flexing at the waist. The front leg is fairly straight and the knee of the rear leg is bent, with the heel off the ground in order to pivot without false cue. The quarterback draws the ball from the center and immediately rotates the ball a quarter turn to the right. The ball should be hidden at belt level with elbows in until making the fake.

DIAGRAM 1: Quarterback practices rolling out right and left. He should work on correct footwork, faking, and speed. Diagram 1 shows his correct movement on a play to the right.

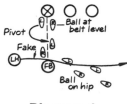

Diagram 1

Fall practice drills: We spend the fall practices on drills that help develop timing, poise, and concentration.

1. Running pass. This drill develops the quarterback's ability to throw the roll-out pass. As shown in Diagram 2, we use two quarterbacks who run in a circular path, going both clockwise and counter-

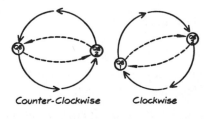

Counter-Clockwise   Clockwise

Diagram 2

clockwise. We start at 20 yards and increase the diameter of the circle. Quarterbacks work on footwork, wrist snap, and proper lead pass.

2. Concentration. The object here is to provide the passer with practice in concentration while under pressure. Using an offensive and defensive end and linebacker, the passer drops back exactly 8 yards and steps up and throws at 6 yards. The ball is thrown to the offensive end in the hook zone as he averts the linebacker. The defensive end rushes the quarterback with arms extended and tries to disrupt the concentration of the quarterback. See Diagram 3.

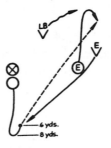

Diagram 3

3. Hitting open receiver. Here we drill to develop the quarterback's ability to hit the open receiver.

> EXECUTION: The following offensive and defensive players are needed: quarterback, three backs, and an end; cornerback, deep halfback, and a linebacker. The drill helps the quarterback view the entire pass coverage before throwing the ball. The quarterback should sprint out and look for primary receivers first (Diagram 4). If covered, he throws the ball to the secondary receiver (Diagram 4a).

4. Lead pass. The object of this drill is to acquaint the quarterback with the speed of all receivers and to provide practice in leading the receiver. The drill needs a quarterback, defender, and receivers. Quarterback calls pass route of receiver and defender plays man-to-man coverage. Quarterback works on footwork, speed to "point of pass," and proper lead pass. See Diagram 5.

> NOTE: Two rules must be followed: On a deep-pass pattern the ball must never be underthrown; on roll-out

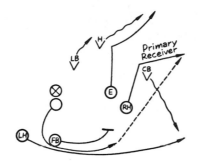

Diagram 4

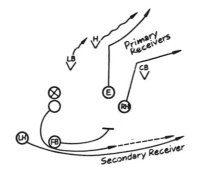

Diagram 4a

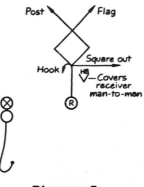

Diagram 5

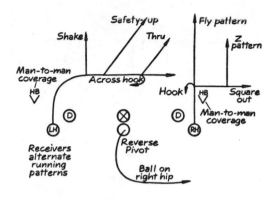

Diagram 5a

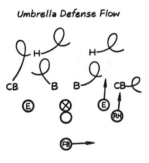

Diagram 6

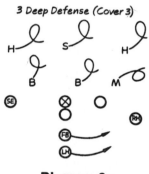

Diagram 6a

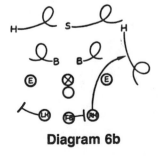

Diagram 6b

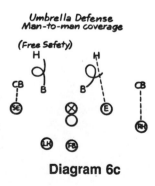

Diagram 6c

passes, the ball should be thrown when receiver is equal to defender.

5. Passing under game conditions. This drill presents types of pass coverage that the quarterback will be confronted with in a game. It is also useful in developing ability to hit the open receiver and in calling the correct play. See Diagram 5a.

Personnel include complete offensive and defensive pass units. The coach calls the down, distance, and time; the quarterback calls play in huddle after receiving the offensive situation. Quarterback is scored on the following: calling correct play (5 points); detecting type of pass coverage being used (4 points); hitting open receiver (3 points); hitting a receiver (1 point).

> NOTE: We use all of our pass patterns in this drill; defensive unit changes its pass coverage every fourth play; this drill has proven most effective in the overall development of our quarterbacks. The defensive and offensive sets are illustrated in Diagrams 6, 6a, 6b, and 6c.

16

Selecting and Developing a Quarterback: Ideas and Drills

by Hub Etchison

Head Football Coach

Richmond (Indiana) High School

Hub Etchison was appointed head football coach and coordinator of Richmond football in 1953. After 21 seasons, his record is 155-52-4. This includes two years as the Number One-ranked team in the state and nine North Central Conference championships. His players and teams have received state and national honors on several occasions.

The quarterback obviously is of first importance to the team. The first consideration of the head coach, therefore, should be the establishment of definite criteria for the selection of the most promising field director. Once chosen, the quarterback should be subjected to an immediate searching training program to ascertain his strongest qualities and further his development.

Selection Criteria

1—The quarterback must be one of the school's foremost athletes and a versatile player, because that is the nature of the position and will be one measure of his ultimate success.

2—He must possess established traits of being a winning athlete, because this reputation will have a tendency to inspire his teammates to greater efforts. Such a player generally is respected for being able to reach his peak under the most intense pressure.

3—The ability to lead a team is essential. This demands a sense of decision and a firm air of command. Personality is involved because the quarterback must be accepted by the team.

4—He must be intelligent enough to think clearly and quickly. The coach must be positive on these points because a player who is lacking may freeze or panic in an emergency.

5—In line with intelligence, the coach should seek a player with a great deal of native football "savvy" and insight into the game. This is because the quarterback is practically an assistant coach, as the liaison man between staff and team.

6—The coach seldom will anticipate finding a great passer, but he must be certain his nominee has displayed some definite ability and success in throwing the football.

Development Program

Responsibility to Provide Smooth Individual Technique

Regardless of the T offense used, the quarterback is 100 per cent responsible for making a smooth fake, handoff, or pitch to his backs, along with getting into positions for passing the football.

It is certain that he cannot be a master in these arts without many hours spent in the practice areas. For that reason, preseason preparation is almost a necessity.

> NOTE: A quarterback, especially a new one, who opens practice obviously awkward and erratic, is not likely to instill confidence, but will raise doubt.

Exchange from center: The coach should begin with the basic move of the ball exchange from center to quarterback. Methods may vary from coach to coach but execution demands perfection. The exchange drill should be a daily practice procedure of 5 to 10 minutes.

Quarterbacks must be expertly trained for a smooth exchange, follow-through with the center, pulling the ball into the pocket, snapping head and shoulders for play action, and stepping to the fake, handoff, pitch, or pass.

> NOTE: I believe procedure and execution can be simplified if the quarterback is taught to look for the spot of responsibility as he commences his execution. The body will follow the eyes.

The drill in Diagram 1 calls for three pairs of centers and quarterbacks (or more) to line up, with one quarterback calling the cadence and all reacting in unison. Quarterbacks rotate so as to exchange with all centers, to become familiar with their manners.

In the drill in Diagram 2, boards are placed in front of the centers with players holding dummies at the ends of the boards. This gimmick

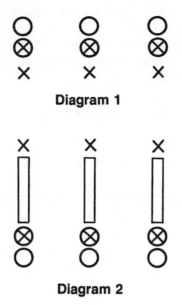

Diagram 1

Diagram 2

offers a more definite hit-out procedure for the center and emphasizes follow-through techniques.

Progression to Team Techniques

Football offenses are confined to inside, off-tackle, and wide plays, and situations must be provided in drills to stimulate all, so that the quarterback may master required techniques.

The inside drill (Diagram 3) will require the quarterback to confine his techniques to inside plays of his offensive group against a live defense. Interior defensive alignments may alter to prove a more complete instructional problem for the quarterback.

> NOTE: To promote competitiveness under pressure, the offense may be required to gain 10 yards in three downs.

The full-line drill will make provisions for the off-tackle and wide plays (Diagram 4). The full-line drill should progress to a full defen-

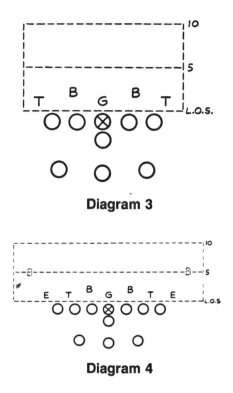

Diagram 3

Diagram 4

sive team as the quarterback advances his expertise. Inside drill procedures may be used to expand the learning scope.

Acquisition of Passing Technique

The ability to throw a football with some measure of success is a
basic factor in the selection of a quarterback, but a coach must assume
he can improve natural ability with a planned procedure.

Coaches and players can be very opinionated and differ widely in
the basic mechanics of throwing, but there are a large number of
excellent drills to promote throwing action of the wrist, arm, and
shoulder. I feel that individual drills are mere supplements of comple-
tion drills to a receiver.

> DRILL 1—Throw quickly to receiver at 7 yards or less
> to emphasize readiness of throwing action (Diagram
> 5).

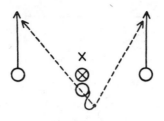

Diagram 5

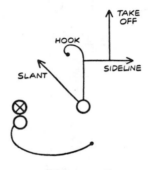

Diagram 6

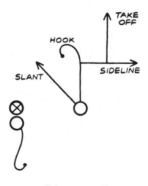

Diagram 7

DRILL 2—Roll-out action with throw on the run to emphasize anticipation of various pass routes of receivers (Diagram 6).

DRILL 3—Drop-back action and throw from set position to emphasize anticipation from the inside position (Diagram 7).

Studying Defense Recognitions

The coach must conduct chalkboard drills, review films, and organize meetings generally to orient the quarterback on the who, how, and why of opposing defenses.

In Diagram 8 the corner drill is opposed by a four-deep arrangement. The scouting report will dictate the basic lineup with adjustments to various formations and types of coverage against the run and the pass.

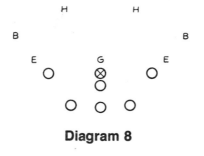

Diagram 8

The seven men on or near the line of scrimmage must cover the internal attack directly, and the quarterback then must learn to recognize the four-man adjustments to flanker, split ends, and man-in-motion formations.

> NOTE: Scouting reports will determine zone, man-for-man, combination, and invert principles.

In Diagram 9, the corner drill is pitted against three-deep defense which comprises four-deep defenses that are rotated or go with flow of

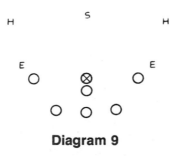

Diagram 9

action. This defense supports an eight-man front, with the halfbacks supporting the ends to check the wide game.

For internal spacing instruction, the inside and full line drills are best. The outside drill teaches the wide run and pass coverages.

Part II

DEFENSIVE DRILLS

1

Motivation Drills for Defensive Football

by Grey Boyles

Head Football Coach

Sparta (North Carolina) High School

Grey Boyles has been coaching high school football for the past 12 years—the last five as head football coach at Sparta (No. Car.) High School, where his squads led the conference in total defense for four years. Before coming to Sparta High School, Coach Boyles was defensive coach at Seminole (Fla.) High School. His overall record to date is 83-50-5.

It's my feelings that a boy must have fun and really enjoy football or he will not respond to coaching, and this is particularly true when it comes to the defensive part of the game.

> NOTE: Our drills are designed to produce strong defensive players—we stress reaction and quick feet —and we manage to make room for some fun and enjoyment while getting the job done

Here are some drills that have helped our program over the years.

Diagram 1 illustrates one fun drill we use. We paint a line

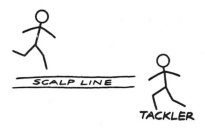

SCALP LINE

TACKLER

Diagram 1

outside of the gym and call it our "scalp line." The first boy dressed and outside gets to tackle the second man out; this continues until everyone is out of the dressing room and onto the field.

NOTE: In its way the drill teaches reaction and quickness. A player is fair game as soon as he opens the door.

Diagram 2 illustrates our ''word of the week'' drill. Our ''word of the week'' (*Blood* for example) helps to key up the players for certain games and teams. The word can be called out at any time during practice, and when the call is made everyone blocks the nearest player to him.

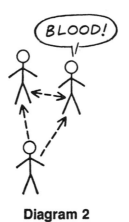

Diagram 2

NOTE: This drill really develops peripheral vision. You can get hit from both sides in the drill so you must react.

Diagram 3 shows a reaction drill for lateral movement (the ''monkey'' drill). Most teams lay down three or four dummies and have the player move laterally over the dummies. We use players instead because it definitely teaches quicker feet and reaction. As in other drills, we use a football to teach movement with a ball.

Diagram 3

Diagram 4 illustrates our "pursuit" drill. We use seven against seven and one runner. The coach points the way for the runner to go, and all defensive players must be on him within five seconds or do push-ups or whatever the offensive players wish.

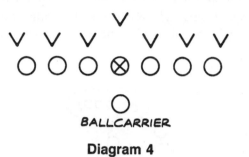

BALLCARRIER

Diagram 4

NOTE: If the defensive team gets to the ballcarrier, then the offensive team must do push-ups or whatever. It's an excellent drill for gang tackling.

Diagram 5 shows a dual drill for toughness and proper tackling. Two players face each other about 2 yards apart. One player has the football, and on the whistle they meet.

BALL-
CARRIER   TACKLER

Diagram 5

NOTE: Each player must make three good tackles or he goes until he does.

Diagram 6 illustrates our "goal-line" drill. We start on the 5-yard line and work down to the 1-foot line. One ballcarrier runs against two defensive players and tries to score. Blockers and defensive players can be added as the coach wishes. All players must stay within a 10-yard box.

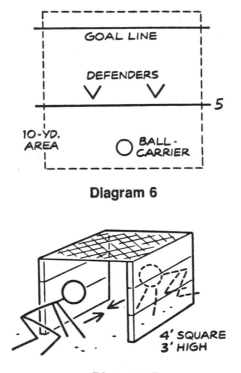

Diagram 6

Diagram 7

Diagram 7 shows our "table" drill. A box 4 feet square and 3 feet high is used. A plank is placed on the side and heavy wire mounted on the top. Both ends are open and two players get down in a four-point stance, charging together on the whistle. A player must go forward or be pushed out of the chute. All the defensive players encourage both boys.

2

Drills to Build Confidence in Your Defensive Team

by Ulysses S. Grant

Head Football Coach

University of Arkansas at Pine Bluff

Ulysses S. Grant has been coaching high school and college football since 1950. In seven years at T.W. Daniel (Crossett, Ark.) High School, he compiled a record of 59-9-2 and three championships; in four years at Southeast (Pine Bluff, Ark.) High School, he posted a 38-12-2 mark and one championship; at the present time, he is head football coach at the University of Arkansas at Pine Bluff (formerly Arkansas A.M. & N. College).

Desire to stop your opponents, plus fundamentals and variety, are the key-notes of success in defensive football. I believe that defensive football is reaction, recognition, and pursuit—and to develop these qualities in your defensive squad, you must first build up their confidence.

> NOTE: Very little acclaim falls to the men whose sole duty it is to stop the enemy, yet without such men no team would ever succeed. It takes a great deal of character and fortitude to be always ready, regardless of the situation, to run onto the field and do your utmost to prevent the opponent from scoring.

Let your boys know this—that they form the backbone of any team when the chips are down (and even when they're not). It's a great start toward building that necessary confidence.

Desire and confidence: For success in any endeavor you must have desire and confidence. Some have it by nature, and in others you must build it. In our practice sessions, I stress concentration, determination, and aggressive attitude—which in turn builds desire and confidence.

Confidence is gained through a series of successes and failures. The fear of failing can cause failures—and a boy must not fear failing at anything. I try not to ever let a boy leave a drill without some measure of success, because we want to emphasize to him how good he can be if he works hard.

> TIP: Attitude, of course, is a tremendous factor in all athletic events. A lot of the attitude business comes about through pride in accomplishment—which again builds confidence.

Our defensive players must learn to strike and attack through certain objects at top speed—and to get to the ball as efficiently as possible. They must be drilled to do this and only this. There is quite a feeling when you get into a game and find that what you are facing is something that you have seen and heard in practice. What a confidence factor!

Selling the defense: For a defense to be successful, it must be sold to your players. Selling is extremely important if you are going to be a strong, sound, defensive team. A person will only do something extremely well when he firmly understands and believes in it. The players must know the general theory of the defense and what it's designed to do.

They must also know the absolute about their specific position. There must be no doubt in their minds as to what their job is; what they are designated to stop; what their area of responsibility is; what specifically they must master.

Your players pick up enthusiasm about the defense from you, and they must learn to "believe" in it the same way you do. Be sure that when you go to them with the defense, you know and believe in it. A sharp bunch of athletes are soon able to catch on to a coach who does not know what he's talking about. If this happens, you've lost the battle.

Practice sessions: One half of our practice sessions are devoted to drills that are broken down into categories—fundamental drills; technique drills; situation drills; group drills. They are designed to build confidence in our defensive men.

Technique Drills

Form tackling drill: For this drill (Diagram 1), we take alternating turns in pairs. One player is a ball carrier and runs first straight, then left and right. The tackler aims the nose in the numbers, dips, and hits by slamming the nose in the numbers and driving the arms around the waist. He lifts by driving the pelvis into the ball carrier—and drives with his legs.

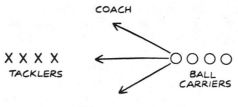

Diagram 1

NOTE: We repeat the above drill with the ball carrier starting in one of those three directions. After being hit and lifted, he is thrown back to his feet. When he lands, he immediately goes in a second direction. This is repeated in a third direction—then the players alternate positions.

Skate tackle drill: To learn to strike without being distracted from the basic function of getting in on the tackle, we set up as shown in Diagram 2. Player A is an offensive blocker at (1) and (2) gaps—at the third gap he becomes the ball carrier, and is form tackled. B must pop the blocker at (1) and (2) and tackle at (3).

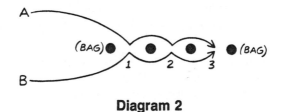

Diagram 2

Fundamental Drills

Eye opener drill: In this drill (Diagram 3), we emphasize that at the corner—the players who get there first with the most enthusiasm will control the game. Players (A) and (B) await the toss of the ball, which determines the offense and defense. Upon the pitch, all four men storm between the dummies and fight to either gain or prevent a gain of 3 yards.

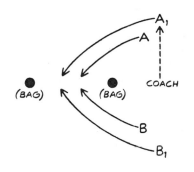

Diagram 3

COACHING POINT: This drill is highly competitive—so we have championships and challenges afterwards. If a boy likes to move and collide, it will show up here early.

Gut test drill: Setting up as shown in Diagram 4, the blockers just try and dig them out and the ball carrier runs as hard as he can. Again, yardage can be measured and champions declared.

TIP: Stunt groups can be drilled well in this manner.

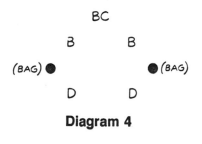

Diagram 4

Group Drills

Gap reaction drill: We start off this section with gap reaction work. We place the player in a gap opposite a ball carrier or key. He must attack one side or the other—then as the key indicates direction, he must get to the ball.

NOTE: We try to react to keys and feel pressure by repetitive drill.

Forcing unit drill: Next we line up the full forcing unit (Diagram 5) in their stances facing the coach 5 yards from the ball. The coach snaps the ball, makes a quick direction move to allow shadow movement—then he tosses or passes the ball.

NOTE: We try to cover quickly all the various defenses we plan to employ on game day.

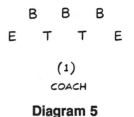

Diagram 5

Pursuit drill: We then progress into a pursuit-type drill as shown in Diagram 6. From this, we learn to beat one-on-one, down blocking, and pass blocking.

NOTE: The coach signals the blocking to be used—the key corresponding to the call.

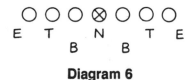

Diagram 6

Situation Drills

Group situation drill: The final 10 to 12 minutes of group drill are often spent on what we call situation drills by groups. Our groups are ends and tackles and linebackers and nose guards. We try to drill against splits, frequency of plays, and technique or schemes the opponents will be using to attack a particular group's area. Each defense and stunt is used.

NOTE: We stress to the players that we are only going to develop as far as the competition in this type of drill forces us to.

Conclusion

These are some of the drills we employ to build confidence in our defensive men—of course, there are more. They are selected and used as to need rather than repeated daily. The important thing is that our boys know it takes hard work to gain confidence.

3

Defensive Football:
Techniques and Drills

by Ken Castles

Head Football Coach

Oak Grove (San Jose, California) High School

Ken Castles' two-year record as head football coach at
Oak Grove (San Jose, Calif.) High School is 19-3. Before coming to Oak Grove, Coach Castles spent two
years at James Lick (San Jose, Calif.) as defensive
coach. The school had a two-year record of 16-2. Before James Lick, Coach Castles was the head football
coach at Liberty (Brentwood, Calif.) High School, with a
four-year record of 26-7-3.

It's our belief that a strong defense is the biggest attribute a team can have. At Liberty High School, we train each player to believe that he is the best, and that no one person can beat him man-for-man. Once we establish this feeling, half the battle is won. It takes great desire and spirit on the part of the boy—and the following defensive techniques and drills help build that desire and spirit.

TWO BASIC DEFENSES: We use two basic defenses, 5-4 and 6-1, with three basic defensive moves —control, fire, and blitz. Let's look at each one.

Control: In a control situation (long yardage), we expect to give the offense 2 to 3 yards per carry. We stress that over-penetration, unless a pass shows, is the worst move we can make. In teaching control, we emphasize these points: (a) watch offensive man's helmet and move with it; (b) work through the offensive player, not around him; (c) stop the charge of the offensive lineman by standing him up with the forearm shiver; (d) the importance of delivering the punch, not catching it from the opponent, is emphasized—when this is done, locate the ball and pursue down the line of scrimmage.

NOTE: When we run into teams that are bigger than we are, control is more difficult. Thus, when the opposition begins to move with consistency, we call for a fire defense.

Fire: This is basically the same as control, with the exception of one move. The defensive lineman now charges at the man in front of

138

him and tries to replace the offensive man's footsteps, while at the same time neutralizing his power. The charge must be made quickly and forcefully as the ball is snapped. He then locates the ball, not penetrating any further than the offensive man's footsteps—for a wild, reckless surge often results in the defensive man being trapped. This initial charge should be controlled.

> OBJECTIVES: When employing the fire defense, the lineman has two immediate objectives: (a) completely overcoming the man across the line of scrimmage; (b) recovering immediately and diagnosing the play. We frequently use this defense in close yardage situations.

Blitz: Diagram 1 illustrates our 50 Blitz. As indicated, the success of this maneuver depends a great deal on teamwork between the tackle and linebackers. The tackle's initial move is important in setting up the offensive lineman so that there's room for the blitzing linebackers to slice through into the backfield. We'll occasionally shoot the weak-side cornerman; the end on that side takes a step in, gets a piece of the end, then drops back into pass rotation. This has proven very successful in passing situations since it confuses the offensive lineman in carrying out rule blocking.

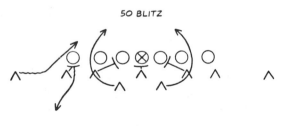

50 BLITZ

Diagram 1

Diagram 2 illustrates our 60 Blitz. The tackles have an important job in cutting off the end. The ends assume the cornerbacks' job on the blitz. The linebackers will jump in the line at the last possible second. A good scouting report will give us the information needed for this blitz to work effectively (rhythm of signal calls, etc.).

Pursuit drill: Diagram 3 illustrates our pursuit drill, which can be very brutal if the coach so desires. The defensive linemen line up in a 50 defense. On the whistle, they fall on the ground, then immediately

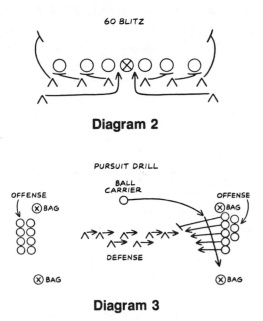

Diagram 2

Diagram 3

jump up to locate the ball carrier, using the proper angle of pursuit. The offensive team on the boundary lines starts on the whistle toward a designated opponent. They try to peel back on the defensive linemen. If we find a defensive lineman not pursuing properly, we send two men to block him. After running this drill a few times, we give any player who gets through to make a tackle a chance to join the offensive team.

> OBJECTIVES: This drill develops (a) quick reactions in locating the ball carrier; (b) proper angle of pursuit; (c) ability to penetrate through blockers; (d) techniques of downfield blocking; (e) desire to be in on every tackle. Naturally, one man can't make every tackle, but he's a better defensive player if he thinks he can

Explode drill: This drill proved to be a great aid for those players who are a little passive when exposed to contact. We make sure players do the drill each day until they begin hitting back instead of catching the blocker. Five-by-five squares are chalked off on the field as illustrated in Diagram 4. A starting line for two offensive linemen is drawn 10 yards from the squares. The defensive man stations himself inside the square and prepares for battle; it's his job to (a) get in a crouch

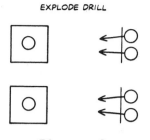

EXPLODE DRILL

Diagram 4

position, ready to recoil; (b) pick out one of the two men (he can't defeat both at the same time); (c) wait until the last possible second and then explode on one of the two offensive players.

> NOTE: The defensive player must stay in the square or he loses the battle. Both offensive men aim their helmets for the defensive man's chest—then try to run through him, making it difficult for him to sidestep both men.

4

Ideas and Drills for Training Crashing Ends

by Gary Sperber

Head Football Coach

Holyoke (Colorado) High School

Gary Sperber began his stay at Holyoke High School as an assistant coach, where his defensive assignment included the training of ends and linebackers. For the past four years, he has been head football coach at Holyoke. His overall mark is 23-13-1, and includes a first and second place in the conference.

All football coaches want the most effective defensive ends possible. To achieve this effectiveness at Holyoke, we train our ends to crash. We feel that this technique has been a great aid to our overall defense for the following reasons:

—It places all 11 men on defense, since our ends will be either in on the tackle or in an angle of pursuit.

—The technique minimizes the chance for a long pass, as the passer has little time to throw.

—The crashing end's attack is difficult to block with pulling guards or trapping tackles because of his penetration.

—The constant pressure applied on the offense by the ends eventually forces mistakes on their part.

—The principle of this technique is easy to teach as far as reading keys is concerned: Our ends are told that they have one unvarying assignment—to *crash*!

Basic Considerations

Personnel: The ideal crashing end is someone with speed, maneuverability, and the desire to make the tackle no matter where the play goes.

> NOTE: Due to the amount of running required of this man, we prefer someone who is not a starter on offense.

Stance: After trying several different stances, we settled on a four-point sprinter's stance. We found that there were two distinct advantages to this: there is a great deal of speed from the start as well as a lack of any problem in maneuverability, as the end is running straight into the opposing backfield.

Alignments

We have come up with a basic alignment with certain modifications to meet any offensive situation.

Normal alignment: Here, our end places himself from 2 to 5 yards outside the offensive end, facing both the ball and the offensive backfield, as shown in Diagram 1. The end should be on an angle that would place him about 1 yard in front of the near back if each ran straight ahead.

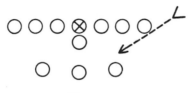

Diagram 1

ADVANTAGES: The end is looking into the backfield and at the ball at the same time, helping to force the offense to run inside the line. Additionally, the end doesn't have to cut as sharply when pursuing down the line. Finally, this angle makes it difficult for pulling guards and trapping tackles to block our defensive ends.

Slot back: The alignment is the same as above, provided the offensive end splits more than 5 yards. If he doesn't split far enough to allow us to get through, the end lines up outside him and narrows his angle of attack, as seen in Diagram 2.

NOTE: The procedure versus a wingman is to play him as though he were an end, again narrowing the angle of attack.

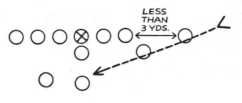

Diagram 2

Unbalanced line: Nothing is changed in the alignment to an unbalanced line but the angle of attack. Because of the position of the near backs, the end on the strong side narrows his angle and the end on the weak side widens his.

Teaching the Techniques

In training a crashing end, you have to prepare him for defense against the same kinds of situations you would train a boxing or static end for.

> A BLOW ON THE GO: The crashing end must be able to locate the ball quickly and react immediately, taking the proper angle of pursuit, eliminating the interference by "landing a blow on the go," and applying every effort to get to the ball quickly. Obviously, he must know how to attack a passer as well as a carrier.

To stop various plays, we have applied the following techniques to each.

The sweep or run-pass option: To attack the sweep away from them, our crashing ends are told to take the best angle of pursuit possible, *not* to follow the path of the ball carrier.

Instead of being responsible for outside containment, our onside end is instructed to whip the interference (the blow on the go), and get to the ball carrier. This forces the interference to belly deeper than they normally would on a sweep, allowing our other end and our linemen to get in pursuit.

> NOTE: Sweeps are often stopped by our offside end coming across to make the tackle from behind.

Off-tackle play: This play is stopped pretty well by the technique of the crashing end, as the angle of attack is very close to the seam of the off-tackle hole.

Plays up the middle: Here our ends are told to "land a blow on the go" with the inside shoulder on any man in the cup protection as they run through him to attack the passer. By using the inside shoulder, the end can make certain that if the passer runs, it must be up the middle, not on the outside.

> ATTACK: Our ends are instructed that they must attack the passer from the top down, never allowing a pass to be thrown with clear vision.

The reverse: Defense against the reverse is probably one of the hardest things to teach the crashing end. In most instances, the other players on the opposite end will have to read the play and communicate it to the end in the direction of the reverse, whereupon that end must react at once to make the play. Scouting reports and offensive sets will usually indicate this possibility, and defensive game preparation with this in mind will help.

Drills

To train our crashing ends to react to these various situations and employ these different techniques, we use a number of specific drills:

Beginning: The best starting drill for checking stance, communication, maneuverability, and pursuit is illustrated in Diagram 3. The ball is hiked to the coach, who quickly throws the ball into the area that the play would go: outside for sweep, up the middle, off-tackle, or drop-back pass. By using this simple drill, the end will quickly learn to start, read the play, communicate it, and react accordingly.

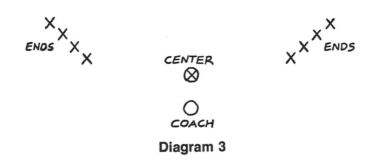

Diagram 3

Landing a blow on the go: We use three drills to instill this principle in our ends.

1. One man holds an air dummy which the crashing end must hit while running through it.

2. The end practices hitting a two-man sled with either a hand shiver or forearm, rolling off and making the tackle on a dummy.

3. To learn how to attack, wipe out the interference, and go after the passer, we have a special drill. With air dummies protecting the passer, the end must hit, protect to the outside, and still get the passer by attacking from the top down. In this drill, the proper positioning of the air dummies is essential.

Angles of pursuit: To further train our ends to read plays and react, we put in a backfield and use plays representing the various situations mentioned previously.

Stopping the sweep: This drill is performed by using two or three people to carry air dummies and run interference for a ball carrier. As the dummies lead the interference, the end must attack and "land a blow" on them, either fighting through or rolling off to make the tackle. The end's minimum effort is to destroy the interference.

5

Drills for Defensive Line Play

by Nick Kotys and Jack McCloskey

Athletic Director and Assistant Football Coach

Coral Gables (Florida) High School

Nick Kotys has been coaching football since 1936, and except for four years (1949-52) as backfield coach under Herman Hickman at Yale, all of it has been at the high school level. At Coral Gables High School since 1952, he has compiled an overall record of 166-30-6 with three state championships. In 1972, Nick Kotys retired from coaching to devote full time to the job of athletic director. Jack McCloskey remains on his staff as defensive coordinator.

We coach our defensive line play within a framework of drills designed to relate to what our boys will meet in a game. I will discuss a few of them here.

Tackling, of course, is first in our defensive thinking; this is the first thing we do. In the first few days of practice we use the circle method, and then switch to the line method (Diagram 1).

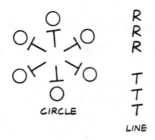

CIRCLE   LINE

Diagram 1

NOTE: In spring and pre-season practice, we tackle at full speed; once the season starts we do mostly form work.

We start by placing the boys in what we feel is proper tackling position, check each one, then have them lift and carry the opponent 5 yards. We start with a pair at a time, so that we may check faults and have the others profit by the corrections. Once they understand what we want, we have them walk at each other and lift and carry; they will move at half speed.

> FULL SPEED: When we get to full speed, we never get more than 5 yards apart, and rarely meet head-on. We would rather do our "live" tackling in the drills, such as the hamburger, three-unity, and others described below.

We feel that work on the seven-man sled (our "monster") is an excellent training aid or "second coach" in teaching our techniques, and the best preparation for our drills. We place the boys in good defensive stance next to the hitting pads and demonstrate the technique of delivering a blow, stepping with proper balance, movement of legs, getting off the block, and pursuit to the ball.

> "BLINDERS": Probably the hardest teaching point is to avoid looking into the backfield until the ball is snapped.We want our defensive linemen to play as if they had blinders on until they feel pressure.

Here are some of our favorite drills:

Hamburger: This is our first drill with a ball carrier, and it follows in our sequence the normal one-on-one and two-on-one drills. We like to lead into it with the offensive man dummy and the ball carrier and tackler live. Then we have the blocker live and the defender making a form tackle. Finally, all are "go." (Diagram 2.)

Diagram 2

> NOTE: This is one of the most fundamental defensive drills. On most plays, the defender must get free of his blocker and make the tackle.

Triple hamburger: This teaches the same technique but we have a backfield and six men working. Generally we set up tackle v. tackle,

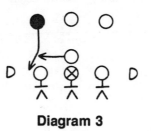

Diagram 3

centers and guards v. centers and guards, and ends v. ends (Diagram 3).

NOTE: We stress gang tackling in this drill.

Three unit: In this drill, we stress the responsibilities of defense. We set up this way (Diagram 4): Left tackles and ends with backfield in one area; right tackles and ends with backfield in another area. The drill is tough on the backfields because they get little rest. This is a half-hour drill, usually, with the backs spending 10 minutes at each station. The drill is good for the three middle men in the line.

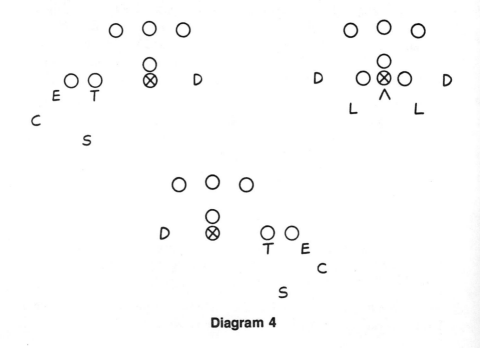

Diagram 4

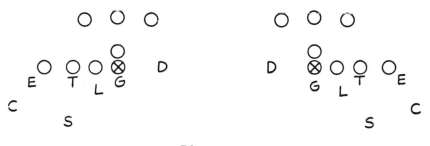

Diagram 5

Half-line: In this drill we use all of our defensive maneuvers and tricks. It is true that the defense has the advantage because they know the direction of the ball; however it builds confidence and makes the offensive blockers work harder (Diagram 5).

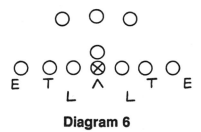

Diagram 6

Eleven on seven: We use a red dog backfield and the first defensive line against the first defensive line (Diagram 6). This is used when the backs are working on pass offense and defense, and for working on our pass rush and recognition of draws and screens.

6

Syracuse Linebacker Drills

by Floyd "Ben" Schwartzwalder

Former Head Football Coach
Syracuse (New York) University

Ben Schwartzwalder retired from coaching in 1973, and left behind one of the most successful coaching careers in the game. An overall mark of 146-76-3 and 25 nonlosing seasons are just part of it. His teams have won a national championship, four Lambert Trophies, and participated in seven bowl games. Ben is a past president of the American Football Coaches Association and is presently serving on the Board of Trustees.

Your linebackers may well be the most important men on your team. They are the key to *any* good defense. And all coaches realize that they can't field a winning football team without having strong defenses.

> THE LINEBACKER: The coach must pick his most aggressive, mobile football players for this important assignment. In order to get maximum value from these men, he must drill them daily in the fundamentals of linebacking—tackling, shedding blockers, and defending against pass plays.

Here are the drills we use at Syracuse to teach aggressive defensive play to our linebackers:

Tackling Drills

> FORM: In all tackling drills, you must stress head behind hands—squared-off body stance. The linebacker must hook the ball carrier into pocket formed by base of neck and inner shoulder. On contact, the tackler swings his arms up and around and locks them. The leg lift is used to get maximum power in the tackle. Linebacker must hit ball carrier in the bread basket.

Inside tackle play: In this drill, we line our men up as shown in Diagram 1. On cue, the ball carrier runs to either side of the dummy.

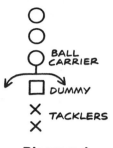

Diagram 1

The tackler (a linebacker) must react to the play and tackle the ball carrier using inside techniques.

Outside tackle play: Our men line up in much the same way as for the inside play. The difference, as you can see in Diagram 2, is that we use two dummies placed 5 yards apart. The ball carrier can run to either end and the tackler makes his tackle using outside techniques. This drill teaches the linebacker to react quickly to plays around the end and familiarizes him with the outside tackling techniques.

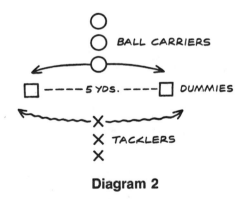

Diagram 2

Variation drills: Using our basic set-up, illustrated in Diagrams 1 and 2, we have two variations on the tackling form drill. In the first, the tackler picks up the ball carrier on his shoulder and digs him back 5 yards before setting him down. The second is the same as the first except that both the ball and the tackler are on the ground. On signal, the ball carrier picks up the ball and the tackler gets off his back, makes the tackle, and digs the ball carrier back 5 yards. Both drills develop leg and arm lift as well as overall strength and coordination.

Shed Blocker Drills

FORM: In all drills, linebackers must assume good football position—crouched square to line of scrimmage with hands in front of body. We stress stepping with the inside foot and hitting with an inside forearm lift. The opposite hand is used for control and added power. Linebackers must not run around blockers —they must control the blocker and go to the ball carrier quickly. All of these drills can be used half speed for form, or from three-quarters to full-out for practice.

Shed blocker and tackle (inside play): Place stand-up dummies 5 yards apart as in Diagram 3. Have tackler line up between dummies 1 to 2 yards from blocker. Ball carrier is 3 yards from blocker. This drill teaches the linebacker to shed blocker and react to ball carrier quickly. It also drills him in inside tackling techniques.

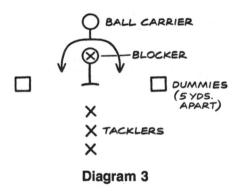

Diagram 3

Shed blocker and tackle (outside play): The set-up is the same as the inside shed blocker drill except that two more dummies are placed to either the right or left side of center (Diagram 4). The drill teaches quick reaction and drills the linebacker in outside tackling techniques.

Shed blocker drill (reaction): Line up four linebackers, four blockers, and a ball carrier as shown in Diagram 5. Keep linebackers 1

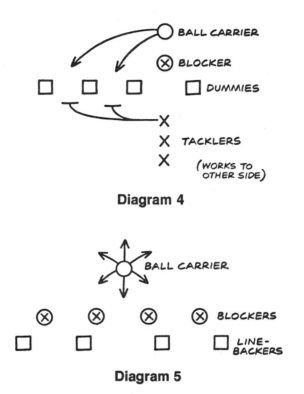

Diagram 4

Diagram 5

yard from blockers and on the outside shoulder. The ball carrier may run in any direction or drop back and set up for a pass. The linebackers must strike a blow on blockers and react to the ball carrier. The ball carrier may start with the ball on command or the coach can use a center and quarterback snap with a pitch or handoff to the ball carrier. This drill teaches quick reaction and agility since the linebackers must react to every movement of the ball carrier.

General Linebacker's Drills

Bull in the ring: Form a circle 5 yards in diameter. Place a linebacker in the center of six equally spaced blockers as in Diagram 6. The linebacker assumes a "ready" or hitting position with feet pumping. The coach can call numbers for the blockers to attack the linebacker or they can attack on their own. If they attack the linebacker from the rear, they must call to him and not hit him until he has turned

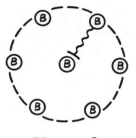

Diagram 6

and is in position to defend. The linebacker sheds blocker and then prepares to take on the next blocker.

> NOTE: We make this strictly a reaction drill and do not
> let the blockers completely unload on the linebacker.

Triangle drill: Place linebacker between two offensive linemen a yard away. The coach signals a lineman to attack the linebacker. Linebacker steps with near foot and forearm to shed blocker, keeping squared off. Then both linemen attack linebacker who must get low and split blockers with shoulder and forearms (Diagram 7).

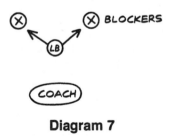

Diagram 7

Position drill: (Diagram 8.) Have passer throw ball between linebackers, who fight for it. This teaches body position as well as quickness and timing. The passer may fake to one group and throw to the other.

Pass reaction drill: Line up receivers 8 yards apart with linebacker 2 yards deep as in Diagram 9. As the ball is snapped, have linebacker retreat, keeping even with the receivers. The linebacker

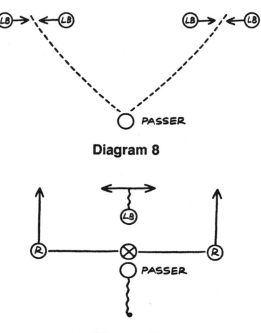

Diagram 8

Diagram 9

must look at the quarterback's eyes and as he starts to throw, must react laterally to the ball. This drill teaches reaction and the value of watching the quarterback's eyes. The linebacker learns to go flat for the ball rather than diagonally. The quarterback can fake ball and run occasionally to keep linebacker more alert.

Depth drill: Have a linebacker in front of each end 2 yards back and a middle linebacker in front of center (Diagram 10). As the ball is snapped, the linebackers on ends can tackle them to prevent them from getting downfield. Linebackers then retreat 10 yards and play the ball. They watch quarterback's eyes and adjust to the position of the receivers. The middle linebacker drops straight back looking for receiver crossing his area. He tries to tackle receiver before ball is thrown. The quarterback may run the ball. If he doesn't, he must throw it before receivers get beyond 15 yards deep.

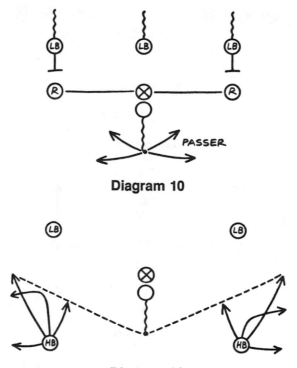

Diagram 10

Diagram 11

Position pass drill: Have passer throw to halfbacks coming out of backfield at different angles as in Diagram 11. This teaches linebackers to assume correct position for each course of release. You must stress that linebacker react quickly to any receiver in the flat. He must watch both the quarterback's eyes and the position of the receiver. Linebacker must block receiver if he comes straight ahead and then react to the ball.

7

Drills for Teaching the Four-Spoke Secondary Defense

by George Pfanner

Head Football Coach

Don Bosco (Ramsey, New Jersey) High School

George Pfanner's record as head football coach at Don Bosco High School is 86-26-2. This includes five state championships and six league titles. He has been voted Coach-of-the-Year four times and All-Star Coach twice.

Much has been written about the 5-4 defense and the secondary that goes with it. Thus, this article will not go into the basics of the defense—but rather it will cover what we look for in personnel to run it, what we hope to teach that personnel, and, most important, how we go about teaching them.

Selection of Personnel

We look for aggressive, quick boys—I say quick as opposed to fast because I feel that a defender is beaten more often when he is retreating or making a lateral move, than on a fly pattern where a high school quarterback is required to throw the ball accurately 40 or 50 yards.

> NOTE: I will now speak on the defense itself, how we adjust it to different situations, and integrate our linebackers into our pass defense.

Personnel alignment: Diagram 1 shows our personnel alignment. The left corner man plays 3 to 4 yards deep and 3 to 4 yards outside the defensive end. The left safety man is 8 to 10 yards deep directly behind our tackle. The right safety is inverted and plays about 6 yards off the ball. We sometimes use this man as a rover, and on an even defense he is required to become a linebacker. This boy should be the best tackler, fast, and aggressive. Our right safety plays 7 yards deep and adjusts to the position of the offensive end. Our linebackers play over the offensive guards about 1½ yards off the ball.

KEYS: The keys for each position are different for each opponent and are worked out from last year's films and this year's scouting reports.

"Now" variation: If we run into a particularly good passing team, we use what we call a "now" variation to our defense (Diagram 2). The reason for calling it "now" is simply that it happens to be easy to call during the game. It consists of several position adjustments.

First, the left corner man is responsible for aggressively attacking the flanker head-on and covering the flat and the end run. The left safety has the flanker deep, or the right end, whoever ends up in his zone. The right safety has middle zone responsibility—and for this reason, we usually change personnel in this spot and use the better pass defender.

The right corner man has the split end man-to-man but gets help from the defensive right end, who lines up head-on and aggressively attacks the offensive end, and then moves inside to cover the run, sprint, or roll-out (Diagram 2).

NOTE: The way we cover the end run is a shade different than the basic 5-4, in that we use the corner man to turn the play in and the safety to be the fill. Other than that we use the basic setup. Diagrams 3 and 4 illustrate these variations.

The linebackers in our defense are depended upon to cover the hook, flat, and swing-type of pattern. The middle guard is responsible for the draw. These general rules hold true only if we are not stunting; if we do stunt, we feel we give up some coverage for the added pressure, and this is a calculated risk determined by our scouting report.

Drill Program

Our philosophy on drills is to take game situations which have given us trouble and work on them through the use of drills. Here are some of them:

Cover the area: This drill (Diagram 5) was designed specifically to teach our defensive secondary just how much yardage could be covered in the time that the ball is in the air.

Basically, the drill is a simple one. Your defensive backs are lined

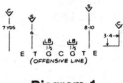

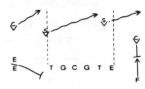

Diagram 1

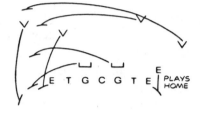

Diagram 2

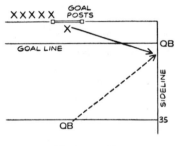

Diagram 3

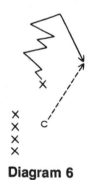

Diagram 4

Diagram 5

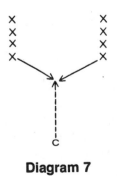

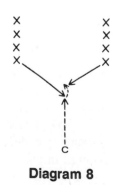

Diagram 6

Diagram 7

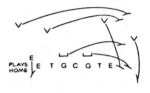

Diagram 8

up between the goalposts. Quarterbacks are placed one at each inter-section of the goal line and the sideline, and one 30 to 35 yards deep directly with the goalposts. As the quarterback turns and cocks his arm, the defensive halfback takes off and sprints to the area where the ball is thrown. The ball is thrown, and the idea is to intercept the ball at the highest point.

> NOTE: In the beginning, it is difficult for the back to get there in time, so the ball is thrown with a good arc and a slight hesitation on the turn by the quarterback—but through constant practice, about mid-way through the season, our quarterbacks can turn and throw without hesitation and very little arc, and the ball will be inter-cepted by the defender.

This drill has helped us a great deal. On two occasions in the past two years, we have had the ball intercepted by a man from another area who had released.

Double-coverage drill: This is another drill for teaching release and coverage. It originates at the sideline with two receivers going downfield running on the yard stripes, 10 yards apart. We have a single defender who is required to cover both receivers. Any pattern can be run but must be run in the same direction.

In other words, if we are going to run a sideline right, both receivers will run the sideline right. If we are going to run a post to the left, both receivers will run a post to the left. As the ball is thrown, it can be thrown to either receiver and the defender must react—whether the ball be thrown in front of him or in back of him. He must react to the ball and intercept it at its highest point.

> NOTE: This is difficult in the beginning, but with con-stant use a boy can and will become adept enough to cover two receivers with a separation of 10 to 15 yards.

It is this type of thinking that causes us to break down the play of the defender into five fundamental areas and try to teach it with a drill. Considering the defensive secondary, we feel that: (1) he must be able to cover a good deal of ground while the ball is in the air; (2) he must be agile enough and fast enough to cover quite a bit of ground while running laterally or backwards; (3) he must aggressively attack the ball; (4) he must be able to get up in the air to intercept the ball; (5) he must be a good open-field tackler.

NOTE: Each of these five areas are covered by one or
more drills.

Reaction drill: This drill (Diagram 6) is designed to teach the
technique of changing direction while running backwards or giving
ground; it's performed individually or by team—usually individually
in the beginning.

A man lines up about 6 yards in front of the coach, and the coach
indicates in which direction he wants the man to run by using a raised
football—back, right, or left. After the man has covered 30 or 40
yards, he is signaled to come back in.

When the ball is thrown for interception, we consider his position
and where the ball would most likely be in his case. If he's a
linebacker, the ball may be thrown low to his left or right; if he's a
defensive safety, it is thrown high to his left or right making him get as
high as possible to intercept the ball.

Fight drill: To practice attacking the ball, we use a fight drill
(Diagram 7). The coach stands on any yard line and has the players
form two lines 20 yards from him, with a separation of about 15 yards
between lines. The coach designates one line as a passing interception
line and the other as a receiving line. The ball is thrown in the middle
of the two lines—it can be either high or low—and the boys go up and
aggressively try to intercept the pass or receive the pass.

Foul-tip drill: The area of getting up and intercepting at the
highest point is taught by use of a foul-tip drill (Diagram 8). Players
line up as in the fight drill—two lines about 15 yards apart and about
20 yards from the coach. One line is the receiving line and the other is
the defending line.

As the coach signals, usually by the cocking of his arm, two boys
come together. The ball is thrown deliberately high; the receiving boy
allows the ball to be tipped through his hands; the defending boy has to
intercept the ball after it has been tipped.

NOTE: It's an excellent drill for teaching very quick
reaction at the moment of possible interception.

Open field tackling is probably one of the most difficult areas to
teach; it is divided into three types of hitting positions—the head-on
tackle; tackle to your right; tackle to your left. Here are the drills we
use for open field tackling.

Spin drill: The spin drill (Diagram 9) is designed to find the ball

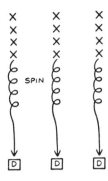

Diagram 9

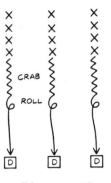

Diagram 10

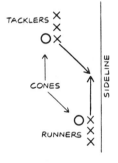

Diagram 11

carrier quickly and then react to his position. At first dummies and then later live players are placed 20 to 25 yards down-field. We use three or four lines so that the most practice can be obtained in the shortest period of time. The boys spin to the right or left as determined by the coach—and upon a whistle or command, straighten out, locate the ball carrier, and with good form pick him up, carry him 2 to 3 yards, and put him down. When we use dummies the tackling is full speed.

Whistle drill: The whistle drill (Diagram 10) lines up the same way—except that the tacklers start in a crabbing position. Upon the whistle they crab downfield, and upon the next whistle are required to roll over, come up in a hitting position, locate the ball carrier, and tackle.

Sideline tackling drill: For this drill (Diagram 11), we place a normal traffic cone 5 to 8 yards from the sideline—and another traffic cone on the sideline 20 yards downfield. The squad is lined up in two groups, one at each cone. The inside group (not on the sideline) is designated the tackling group. Upon a whistle from the coach, the boys proceed—the runner and the tackler.

> NOTE: The coaching point here is to get your head across the body of the ball carrier. The drill is run both to the right and to the left at three-quarters speed.

8

Drills for the Defensive Secondary

by Richard May

Offensive Coordinator
Tennessee Technological University

In four years as head football coach at Jonesboro (Tenn.) High School, Richard May compiled an overall record of 30-8-2, which included three consecutive conference championships. He then moved to Gardner Webb (Boiling Springs, No. Car.) College to serve as defensive coordinator, and next to his present post, offensive coordinator at Tennessee Technological University (Cookeville, Tenn.).

An enormous burden is placed on the defensive secondary because of multiple offensive formations and the complexity of the modern passing attack. It is not realistic to stay with one type of secondary coverage and not expect to be picked apart. The variety of secondary schemes being used today requires the use of drills with constant repetition to teach specific techniques and efficiency in coverage.

I-Line Drill

Diagram 1 illustrates a drill for teaching the technique of moving away from the line of scrimmage using proper footwork to cover potential receivers and playing the ball. The defender assumes the proper stance in a low, coiled position, and on the indicated pass signal from the coach, he yells "pass" and moves away from the line of scrimmage on a straight line. The coach will point the ball in the direction he wishes the defender to cut. The defender will plant his foot, flop his hips, changing sides, and stay low on a straight line. After several cuts, he intercepts the thrown ball at its highest point using an oral interception call.

II-Tip Drill

Diagram 2 illustrates a drill to teach the defender's reaction to a deflected ball. The defender lines up 10 yards directly in front of the coach with a rear defender 5 yards behind the front man. They start

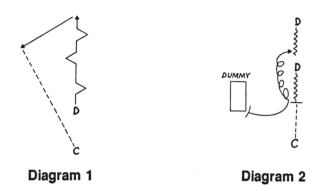

Diagram 1   Diagram 2

running toward the coach, who throws the ball directly over the front man's head. The front man tips the ball to the rear man, who intercepts the ball at its highest point and gives the oral interception call. The front man then blocks the dummy which represents the intended receiver.

III-Zone Drill

Diagram 3 is a drill to teach the defender to play the field and the ball—not the individual receivers—and his reaction to the thrown ball. Two lines of receivers are placed on the hash-marks with the defender in the middle of the field. As the receivers move off the line of scrimmage, the defender keeps a cushion on the receivers from the middle of

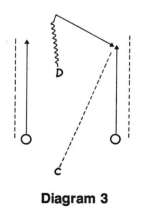

Diagram 3

Diagram 4   **Diagram 5**

his zone and does not flop his hips unless forced to do so. As the defender shuffles back, his eyes fixed on the coach, so as to get a jump on the ball, he intercepts the thrown ball at its highest point using the oral interception call.

IV-M/M Drill

Diagram 4 is a one-on-one drill used to teach man-to-man coverage. The defender covers the receiver one-on-one against any pass route, keeping proper position on the receiver and reacting to the thrown ball.

V-Combat Drill

Diagram 5 illustrates a drill to teach the defender to concentrate on the ball and intercept it in heavy traffic. A group of three defenders are placed approximately 3 yards apart. The coach throws the ball in the middle of the group, the defenders fight for the ball, and one intercepts it at its highest point.

VI-Key

A drill used to teach the defenders to read their keys to determine pass or run is shown in Diagram 6. Place a center, quarterback, running backs, and end in their offensive positions. The defensive cornerback and safety line up in their normal defensive positions and react to

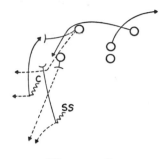

Diagram 6

the movement of the offense. If the end blocks, the cornerback moves up and continues the run with the safety filling head-on on the football. If the key indicates a pass, the cornerback and safety react to their pass responsibilities.

VII-Reaction and Overlap Principle

Diagram 7 illustrates a drill to teach reaction to the ball and the overlap principle in the zones. The defensive secondary and linebackers are placed in their positions and react to their area of responsibility. The coach throws the ball to one of the defenders, and the other defenders react to the ball and get in position to tip it. After all defenders have tipped the ball, the last defender will intercept it at its highest point, and the rest of the defenders will get into position to lead him up the field.

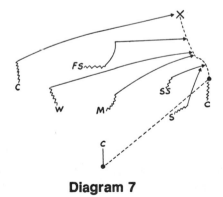

Diagram 7

VIII-Skeleton Drill

Diagram 8 is a drill to coordinate the defensive secondary and linebackers while working on all coverages. A skeleton offensive group is set up to run the opponents' favorite pass routes while the defenders work on all coverages and adjustments to be used.

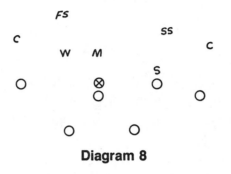

Diagram 8

IX-Form Tackling

Diagram 9 illustrates a drill for form tackling. Defenders are placed in a 5-yard square, and on command the ball carrier runs half speed in the direction of the tackles, not cutting in either direction. The tackler, in a low, coiled position, butts the ball carrier with the front of his helmet with an upward explosion and carries him back 5 yards.

Diagram 9

Diagram 10

X-Meeting Blocker

Diagram 10 demonstrates meeting a blocker, playing him off, and making the tackle. Place two dummies on the ground about 6 yards apart. Have a line of blockers, ball carriers, and tacklers. The ball is thrown to the ball carrier, who tries to evade being tackled. The tackler meets the blocker, playing him off with his hands and making the tackle.

XI-Open-Field Tackling

Diagram 11 illustrates a drill for teaching tackling in the open field. The ball carrier and tackler line up 15 yards apart between the sideline and hash-marks. The ball carrier breaks right or left; the defender sprints to a point 5 yards in front of the ball carrier, breaks down moving his feet and looking at the ball carrier's numbers, and makes the tackle with his head in front.

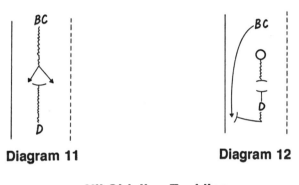

Diagram 11   **Diagram 12**

XII-Sideline Tackling

Diagram 12 shows a drill for teaching the defender to play off the blocker and make the tackle on the sideline. The ball carrier, with the blocker in front of him, is lined up approximately 10 yards apart in a 6-yard lane between the sideline and the hash-mark. On command from the coach, the ball carrier will run, making his cut, and the defender will ward off the blocker, keeping an inside-out position and forcing him out-of-bounds.

9

Two-on-One Tackling Drill

by Gary Sloan

Head Football Coach
New Mexico Thunderbirds

After two years as a graduate assistant at Springfield (Mass.) College, and a year of junior high coaching, Gary Sloan took over the head football job at Hobbs (N. Mex.) High School. His three-year record there was 12-6-2. He next moved to the University of Idaho (as an assistant) and the University of New Mexico (as an assistant). At present, he is head football coach of the New Mexico Thunderbirds, a member of the Southern Professional Football League.

Since we agree with the theory that a drill should represent game situations, we feel our two-on-one tackling drill (with variations) is one of our most important team defensive drills. It helps prepare us for four game situations:

1. Two men converging on a ball carrier.

2. Two men converging on a punt return.

3. Two men converging on a kick-off return.

4. Two men converging on a pass receiver.

We line up for the drill as follows (Diagram 1)·

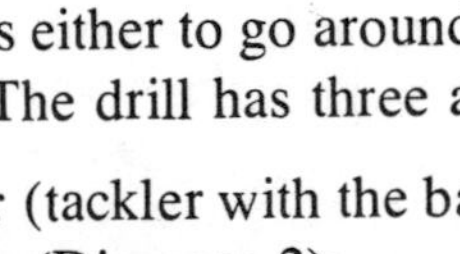

$$T \longleftarrow 8 \text{ YDS.} \longrightarrow T$$

$$\text{(BC)}$$

Diagram 1

The ball carrier tries either to go around the two tacklers, or shoot the gap between them. The drill has three areas of responsibility:

1. *The cut-off man:* (tackler with the ball moving in his direction) has these responsibilities (Diagram 2):

a. Does not let ball carrier around him.
b. Helps on the cut-back.
c. Becomes a gap man when the ball goes opposite him.

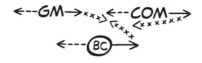

Diagram 2

2. The *gap man* (tackler with ball moving away from him) has these responsibilities (Diagram 3):

   a. Does not let the runner cut the gap between him and the cut-off man.
   b. Becomes cut-off man when the runner reverses and comes to him.
   c. Keeps distance relationship between himself and the cut-off man.

Diagram 3

3. The *ball carrier* should try to move back and forth as much as possible. He may try to hit the gap anytime he feels he has the tacklers out of position (Diagram 4).

Diagram 4

NOTE: You can vary this drill by giving the ball carrier two blockers. The cut-off men have the same responsibility except that now they must play the blocker.

10

The Add-On Tackle Drill

by Bob Cote

Head Football Coach
Thornton (Saco, Maine) Academy

Bob Cote has been coaching high school football for 17 years. At his former post, St. Louis (Biddeford, Me.) High School, his squads captured three state championships and were runners-up twice. At his present post, Thornton (Saco, Me.) Academy, his 1972 squad tied for the conference championship and were runners-up in 1973. His overall coaching record is 111-39-5.

Good tackling requires practice. Last spring I hit on a device that gives us more time for other skills and at the same time gives us more tackling practice than ever before.

It's simply this: I have added an "extra" to many of our standard drills. Instead of finishing as they always have, we have added a tackle to the drill. This gimmick has been used on both group drills and individual drills.

In addition to saving us time and giving us more tackling practice, an examination of the movies of our final scrimmage showed that tackling was much improved. Our boys did not stop after the first effort—they would follow through, involve more men, force more fumbles, and prevent long runs.

Here are a few of our drills. (See accompanying Diagrams.) You see that they are standard drills, and all we have done is add a tackle to the end of each one. All it takes is a little imagination; the possibilities are unlimited.

Defensive men hit the sled and then tackle the first offensive man opposite them. After the tackle, the men involved change lines —defensive becomes offensive and offensive becomes defensive. (Diagram 1.)

Defensive men hit sleds 1, 3, 5, and 7. After contact with each, they spin and run to the next. After hitting the last sled, they spin, pursue, and tackle the offensive man. Again, lines are changed after each sequence. (Diagram 2.)

Defensive men break through blockers and tackle offensive men, who can either remain stationary or move. (Diagram 3.)

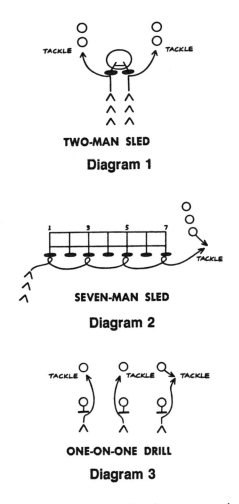

TWO-MAN SLED

Diagram 1

SEVEN-MAN SLED

Diagram 2

ONE-ON-ONE DRILL

Diagram 3

NOTE: In all of the above drills, the runners should not move head-on. They must run on an angle. Runners should move at half-speed.

11

Drills for Developing Tacklers and Blockers

by Les Dunn

Former Head Football Coach

Box Elder (Utah) High School

Les Dunn recently retired from coaching high school football after 22 years. He has an overall winning average of 72% and is a member of the Coaches' Century Club for football, swimming, and track.

The difference between a poor tackler and a good tackler is 1,000 tackles; the difference between a poor blocker and a good blocker is 1,000 blocks.

This is my credo, because I believe football players are made, not born. Blocking and tackling can be taught, and the best taught team in these two basic fundamentals of football has the best chance of success. Thus, my practice schedules are made up with a maximum of blocking and tackling drills.

> AVOID MONOTONY: I know that an hour-and-a-half of blocking and tackling can be monotonous. Therefore, I make my drills as competitive as possible and use a variety of them—and no one drill is run too long.

But drills develop good tacklers and blockers, and here are some I use.

Tackling Drills

We use five basic tackling drills: two for warm-up purposes and three at full speed. *We work all drills, as well as tackling and upright blocking, from the hit position.* This is it, and we spend time each day on it:

> FORM: Spread the feet about shoulder width, with knees flexed and wide, back straight, head up, hands and arms relaxed with the hands inside the knees, palms in. From this position, we work on agility, moving backward, forward, and sideways.

1. Half speed tackling: Tackler assumes hit position yards away from a stationary ball carrier. As the ball carrier makes his move (left or right), the tackler steps in and makes contact waist high with his head in front of or on the ball side of the carrier's body, lifting hard as contact is made to get the ball carrier's feet off the ground and carrying him back about 5 yards. The back is kept straight, head up, and eyes on the target. (Diagram 1.)

Diagram 1

2. Balance tackling: Tackler assumes hit position 10 yards from the ball carrier. On signal, he runs forward to 3 feet of the ball carrier, stops, but keeps feet moving up and down in the hit position. The ball carrier then makes his move to left or right, and the tackler follows the half-speed drill procedure. (Diagram 2.)

Diagram 2

3. Linebacker: Three dummies are lined up a yard apart. The ball carrier is 4 yards in back of the middle dummy; the tackler is in the hit position 2 yards in back of the same dummy. The ball carrier makes his move and breaks to either side of the middle dummy, and the tackler reacts to position himself for the tackle by side-stepping into position in front of the ball carrier. The tackle is made as in the half-speed drill. (Diagram 3.)

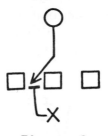

Diagram 3

4. Open-field tackling: Two dummies are set up 5 yards apart. The ball carrier and tackler are lined up 5 yards in back of the space between the dummies. On command, both start forward at the same time, the tackler advancing as in the balance drill, keeping in front of the ball carrier, and making the usual tackle. (Diagram 4.)

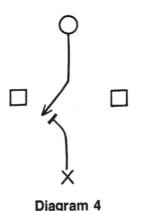

Diagram 4

5. End drill: (This drill emphasizes both tackling and defensive use of the hands.) Two offensive men line up, one a blocker, the other a ball carrier. The defensive man is placed between two dummies (5 yards apart). The defensive man must come across two steps, turn to the inside, and jam the off-tackle hole. He must slip the blocker and meet the back if the back goes wide. He must meet the blocker with a touch hand shiver, low, with the inside foot forward. If the ball carrier tries to go wide, he drives his inside arm between himself and the blocker toward the ball carrier and pursues, making the tackle. (Diagram 5.)

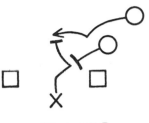

Diagram 5

CONSISTENCY: By following this progression daily, we find that most boys learn to tackle fairly well. The big thing, we feel, is consistency—working on this every day all season.

Blocking Drills

We work our blocking drills from our block position, and this is it:

FORM: Stand with feet spread shoulder width apart, or a little wider, with one foot back (toe to instep). Then squat with heel and toe in line, heels down with elbows on knees, straight back, and head up. Reach out with the hand on the side of the back foot and touch the ground as far in front as possible without falling forward, and then rock forward on the knuckles. Head is up, shoulders squared, back straight, with hips and shoulders level.

1. One-on-one: Blocker drives his head at the numbers just below the face guard of the opponent, extending both legs with explosive power, and bringing the elbow forward to form a cradle with the head. As contact is made, the head slips to the proper side, and the feet come under the body. The lift and drive is hard in an effort to straighten the opponent up and drive him back or to the side, whichever is desired. After the initial drive, the legs must be kept in motion in order not to lose contact. (Diagram 6.)

Diagram 6

NOTE: We start with passive resistance, then progress to full-speed drive.

2. Two-on-one: Two blockers take block position, one being designated as the lead blocker, the other the drive blocker. The lead blocker makes his block as in the one-on-one, making sure his head slips to the *outside*. The drive blocker drives his head at the near hip of the opponent, and proceeds as in the one-on-one, letting his head slip to the outside and making sure that the first step is taken with the inside foot. (Diagram 7.)

Diagram 7

Diagram 8

3. Crowther charging: Two hurdles are set up in front of a two-man sled. A crossbar is placed on the hurdles. Two blockers line up in position in front of the hurdles and crowther. The coach stands behind the blockers with a 1'' x 4'' or a 2'' x 4'', or any other suitable whip. On command, the blockers charge toward the crowther, under the crossbar, and the coach swings the board, hard. It usually only takes one swat to speed up the slowest boy. (Diagram 8.)

4. Board drill: This is a real favorite with us. As a warm-up, we place a dummy in the middle of a 1'' x 12'' board, 10 to 15 feet long. Two blockers line up facing the dummy, feet spread outside the board. On command, both men charge forward, trying to drive both man and dummy off the board. We then remove the dummy, and the men face each other, one designated offense, the other defense. The defensive man tries to throw the offensive man off the board; the offensive man tries to throw the defensive man off or get by him in any way possible. (Diagram 9.)

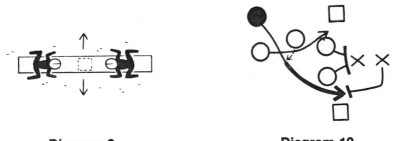

Diagram 9   **Diagram 10**

NOTE: This drill has a high competitive value. The men
like it and it can develop into a real contest.

5. Separator drill: Two dummies are set up 2 yards apart. Two offensive blockers and one defensive man are placed in the hole. A linebacker is placed behind the defensive man. A quarterback and two offensive backs are lined up behind the offensive blockers in position to run cross-bucks or the belly series. The coach stands behind the defense and signals the play and the starting command. The quarterback then takes over and runs the play. The defensive lineman tries to fight through the two-on-one block, and the linebacker must read the block of the offensive linemen, move parallel, and fill the hole, making the tackle on or behind the line. (Diagram 10.)

NOTE: This is an excellent drill which the players like. It
is a game situation drill, and teaches offensive blocking, defensive line play, and linebacker skills.

Naturally, we use many other drills, but these are our fundamentals, and are repeated daily. Once again, I feel that *consistency* is the thing that makes them work and helps us develop good blocking and tackling teams.

Part III

SPECIAL DRILLS

1

Preseason Practice and Drills

by Bob Williams

Head Football Coach
The Choate (Wallingford, Connecticut) School

Bob Williams has been head football coach at The Choate (Wallingford, Conn.) School since 1963. His overall record is 49-23-4.

Ours is a boarding school, so the players live on campus during our ten-day preseason football camp. We house 75 boys and one coach in a dormitory throughout this session.

> NOTE: The obvious advantages of this procedure are being able to control the player's diet and sleep time—but just as important is the feeling of team unity that comes from living and working together. The boys are unanimous in saying that camp is a very meaningful part of their football experience.

Our daily schedule is shown in Chart I.

Schedule details: We open camp three weeks before our first game, which allows us about ten days alone before the remainder of the student body arrives on campus. Since we do not have spring practice, we feel that this period is the minimum needed to prepare for our first game.

> NOTE: Players arrive at camp on a Sunday evening, have their physicals, and get equipment on Monday morning; then they begin their first workout on Monday afternoon. Tuesday through Friday double practices are held, and on Saturday morning we have a controlled scrimmage with another school.

Boys are permitted to go home from Saturday noon to Sunday evening. Early in the second week the same daily schedule is followed, with another controlled scrimmage being held on Wednesday. On Friday, classes start and we change to one practice a day. Camp concludes

```
7:30 AM    — Breakfast
9:00 AM    — Practice
12:00 NOON — Lunch
1:00 PM    — Quarterbacks'
              Meeting
3:30 PM    — Practice
6:30 PM    — Dinner
8:00 PM    — Team Meeting
10:00 PM   — Lights Out
```

Chart I

with a game scrimmage against a neighboring school on Saturday afternoon.

Practice schedule: Each day of camp we have an offensive practice in the morning (Chart II) and a defensive practice in the afternoon (Chart III). Practices are always the same and all workouts are in full equipment.

While the schedule may seem somewhat boring for the players, it does teach football well. Our experience has been that boys prefer working and winning to being entertained and losing.

> NOTE: While we do adjust the lengths of drills somewhat as camp progresses, our basic practices do not vary. After the first few days of camp, a coach has only to call out the name of a drill and his players will group themselves correctly.

Drill instruction: When running a drill, we ask a coach to watch only one man. Since some of our drills are used for both offense and defense, he may watch the blocker in one session and the defender in the other. In large drills such as passing, we have one coach work with the passers and another with the receivers. While this might seem to require a big staff, we are able to handle more than 70 boys with four coaches.

> NOTE: Our practices can actually be run with only three coaches; this allows the head coach to move around the field and observe drills and players.

Line Coach	Backfield Coach	End Coach	Head Coach
9:00 AM Calisthenics – Team	9:00 AM Calisthenics – Team	9:00 AM Calisthenics – Team	9:00 AM Calisthenics – Team
9:10 AM Form Block – 4,5,6	9:10 AM Form Block – Backs	9:10 AM Form Block – 2,3,7,8	9:10 AM Form Block – Backs
9:15 AM 2-Man Sled – 4,5,6	9:15 AM Wilkinson – Backs	9:15 AM 2-Man Sled – 2,3,7,8	9:15 AM Wilkinson – Backs
9:20 AM 7-Man Sled – Line	9:20 AM 2-Man Sled – W,T	9:20 AM 7-Man Sled – Line	9:20 AM 2-Man Sled – Q,F
9:25 AM Scramble – 4,5,6	9:25 AM Techniques – Backs	9:25 AM Scramble – 2,3,7,8	9:25 AM Techniques – Backs
9:40 AM Double-Team – 4,5,6	9:40 AM Block Ends – Backs	9:40 AM Double Team – 2,3,7,8	9:40 AM Block Ends – Backs
9:55 AM Trap – Q,F,4,5	9:55 AM Action Pass – Backs, Ends	9:55 AM Pull – 3,6,7	9:55 AM Action Pass – Backs, Ends
10:10 AM Cup Protection – 4,5,6	10:10 AM Dropback Pass – W,T,2,8	10:10 AM Cup Protection – Q,F,3,7	10:10 AM Dropback Pass – W,T,2,8
10:25 AM Signals – Team	10:25 AM Signals – Team	10:25 AM Signals – Team	10:25 AM Signals – Team
10:50 AM Kick – Team	10:50 AM Kick – Team	10:50 AM Kick – Team	10:50 AM Kick – Team

EQUIPMENT

5 Bags
6 Shields
1 Canvas

OFFENSIVE CODE

2,8 – End
3,7 – Guard
4,6 – Tackle
5 – Center

W – Wingback
Q – Quarterback
F – Fullback
T – Tailback

Chart II

Drill cards: Each coach works with the same positions daily. The line coach, for instance, will work with the offensive tackles and centers in the morning and the defensive tackles and guards in the afternoon.

In all drills, coaches are provided with a large card (Diagram 1) on which the drill has been drawn. As an example, in our scramble drill, the coach will stand behind the defensive player and point out which of the two variations he wants the offense to execute.

Line Coach	Backfield Coach	End Coach	Head Coach
3:30 PM Calisthenics – Team	3:30 PM Calisthenics – Team	3:30 PM Calisthenics – Team	3:30 PM Calisthenics – Team
3:40 PM Agility – G,T	3:40 PM Agility – H,S,M	3:40 PM Agility – L,E	3:40 PM Agility – H,S,M
3:45 PM Form Tackle – G,T	3:45 PM Form Tackle – H,S,M	3:45 PM Form Tackle – L,E	3:45 PM Form Tackle – H,S,M
3:50 PM 2 on 1 – E,T	3:50 PM Piano – H,S,M	3:50 PM Key – L,G	3:50 PM Piano – H,S,M,
	4:00 PM Pass Defense – H,S,M		4:00 PM Pass Defense – H,S,M
4:05 PM 3 on 1 – G,T		4:05 PM Piano – E,L	
4:20 PM Pit – G,T,E		4:20 PM Pass Defense – L	
4:35 PM Open Field Tackle – G,T,E	4:35 PM Open Field Tackle – H,S,M,L	4:35 PM Open Field Tackle – G,T,E	4:35 PM Open Field Tackle – H,S,M,L
4:45 PM Rush and Return – Team	4:45 PM Rush and Return – Team	4:45 PM Rush and Return – Team	4:45 PM Rush and Return – Team
4:55 PM Signals – Team	4:55 PM Signals – Team	4:55 PM Signals – Team	4:55 PM Signals – Team
5:20 PM Condition – Team	5:20 PM Condition – Team	5:20 PM Condition – Team	5:20 PM Condition – Team

EQUIPMENT   **DEFENSIVE CODE**

EQUIPMENT	DEFENSIVE CODE	
5 Bags	G – Guard	H – Halfback
8 Shields	T – Tackle	S – Safety
1 Canvas	E – End	M – Monster
	L – Linebacker	

Chart III

These cards are usually not needed after the first few days of camp, but players find them very helpful during the early sessions. We have found that shirt cardboards are ideal for this purpose.

NOTE: We feel that a boy should be in a contact drill every sixth time it is run. Therefore, for a drill requiring

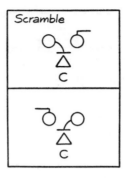

Diagram 1

three players, a group of 18 boys would be ideal. During the first workout shields are used, but following this all drills are live.

Offensive practice: Our offensive practices are set up for the balanced line, single-wing. The only problem which might appear in using this program with the T-formation occurs in the trapping and pulling drills, since our trapper never pulls and our puller never traps.

> NOTE: However, there are many drills available where offensive guards can be taught to both pull and trap.

Defensive practice: The defensive practices are set up for a 5-4 monster defense, but can be adapted easily to other fronts. Our personnel makeup is similar to most high schools, with our players being sophomores, juniors, and seniors in the 15-18 age group. Because of the adjustment problems sometimes encountered in living away from home, we normally do not invite freshmen to camp.

> NOTE: In practices such as these, a good student manager is essential. Our manager is required to time all drills, provide coaches with drill cards, and be sure that required equipment is on the field. Our best managers have been boys who are not athletically inclined. They do the work at hand rather than pass and punt the football during practice.

Throughout our program, we try to keep things safe, simple, and sound. We certainly feel that the preseason program presented here embodies all these principles.

2

New Practice and Drill Techniques

by Harry Billups

Former Head Football Coach
Sherrard (Illinois) High School

Harry Billups' eight-year record as head football coach at Sherrard High School is 46-28-5. This includes three runners-up to the conference title and a conference title in 1970. In 1971, Harry Billups retired from coaching and was appointed principal at Sherrard High School.

Not too many years ago it was considered necessary to carry out football practice to the point of exhaustion. It was felt that the length and severity of the drilling determined the product. In recent years the thinking of many coaches has changed, because it has become known that athletes learn much faster if they are not fatigued from protracted, strenuous practice.

> NOTE: While learning could be acquired in the early course of the all-out drill, this process would break down very rapidly, leaving physical training alone to be gained.

New awareness: There arose a new awareness that the practice tempo and environment are important factors which will affect the squad's attitude toward the coach and the sport, and will certainly affect the possibility of success. Out of this came two terms which define the types of practice techniques followed by most football coaches today.

> 1—Mass practice, which is continuous, with no rest period.
> 2—Distributive practice, which is designed with rest periods scheduled at definite points.

Use of techniques: Each type, mass and distributive, has its advantages, but it is important for a coach to know when to use each one, and to have a keen appreciation of what may be obtained from each. Mass practice is very useful if the skill to be taught is a simple motor act. A four-point stance is an example.

Relearning an act: Any act that once was known may be re-learned faster in a mass practice than in a distributive situation. Also, any technique that must be reviewed from time to time would best be performed in a mass practice. However, the complex motor skills of football, such as the reverse block and the pulling guard techniques, more properly belong in a distributive practice.

> NOTE: In such a practice the coach first explains the skill, has it practiced, calls a halt, and then repeats the process.

Frequency of rests: Coaches often have difficulty deciding how many rest periods should be given, and the duration of each. Some feel that a regimented environment should prevail through practice. The rest periods, in fact, may be disguised so that the athlete is busy mentally, and is not too aware he is taking a break.

> NOTE: One method divides the squad into groups during a rest period, for special instructions from assistant coaches.

Chalk session: A general chalk session with the head coach in charge is another means of permitting rests without idleness. During such sessions ice chips or small quantities of water may be given.

Such treatment and diversity in the rest periods gives the individual a psychological lift and takes the drudgery out of practice.

3

Off-Season Compensating Drills

by Larry McCoy

Athletic Director and Head Football Coach
Athens (Alabama) High School

Larry McCoy started coaching football at Athens High School in 1963 and became head football coach and athletic director in 1966. His overall record is 51-28-2, with 31-9-1 being the record for the past four years. In 1972, Athens went undefeated with a 10-0 mark. Over the past three years, Athens finished in the top ten in the state.

Athens High School has an enrollment of only 500 students in the upper three grades, yet we must compete with schools of 1,500 to 2,500 in those classes.

The resulting disadvantage in depth must be offset, and we coaches believe one good means to compensate is a strong physical development program in the off-season.

> NOTE: This period begins the last week in November and continues to the first week in March, when spring football practice begins. Our state allows spring practice.

Five-day week: Over this period of approximately 15 weeks, we offer a five-day fitness program per week, with one coach supervising the junior high players and three coaches in charge of the varsity.

On Mondays, Wednesdays, and Fridays a one-hour program is set up in quickness patterns, mat drills, and weights; on Tuesdays and Thursdays a like time is devoted to concentration on running.

> NOTE: Since the gym is monopolized by basketball in the football off-season, mats are placed in the two dressing rooms.

Three-Day Schedule

I Exercise
  1- Side straddle hops
  2- Knee bends
  3- Stretch groins

II— Drills (two lines at a time)
    1- Forward roll
    2- Forward roll and wave off mat
    3- Belly flop and wave off mat
    4- All fours across mat
    5- Wave drill with men in football position—right, left, backward, forward
    6- Three-man roll, figure eight (twice)
    7- Nose-on-nose; one leader, two followers (twice)
    8- Charge under a board on sound and movement
    9- Six-at-a-time on mat; coach uses whistle, boys move feet, hit mat front and back up as fast as possible (twice)
    10- Neck bridges
    11- Push-ups, as many as may be done in 1 minute (twice)
    12- Sit-ups, as many as may be done in 1 minute (twice)

III—Wrestling for 1 minute, not trying for a pin, but to keep in motion throughout

IV—Weight Machine (one set with enough weight to do from 6 to 10 repeats)
    1- Curls
    2- Overhead pull
    3- Bench press
    4- Behind neck press
    5- Running track for legs
    6- Chins (10)
    7- Sit-ups (15)
    8- Back dips (5)
    9- Dips for shoulders (5)
    10- Back extensions (5)
    11- Leg table front
    12- Leg table back

V— Power Racks
    1- Dead lift
    2- Heel raises
    3- Half squats

VI—Isometrics (pull all-out for 8 seconds)
    1- Dead lift
    2- Curls
    3- Shoulder pull

4- Squats

5- Standing press

Two-Day Schedule

I— Exercise (same as other days)

II— Hurdles (four low hurdles 20 yards apart, with 20 yards run-in, 20 yards run-out).

III— Sprints

    1- Tuesdays: Two 50's, two 100's, one 220.

    2- Thursdays: Two 100's, one 220, one 440.

IV—Rope climbing, two times each—overhead ladder and chins.

V— Isometrics (same as other days)

Utilizing assets: The coaches believe that the extra hard work in this demanding program makes it possible to utilize all available resources during the off-season, and encourage physical development, and ensure psychological well-being.

> NOTE: In a sweeping effort for all-around upgrading, every effort is made to motivate academic improvement in the off-season.

The program has appealed to the athletes in recent years and gained their wholehearted support as a means to self-improvement. The coaches feel that this desire by the athletes has had a big role in maintaining the tradition that Athens High School always fields a team that is in the running.

4

Football Drills for Selecting Players

by George H. Pinckney, Jr.

Assistant Football Coach

Orange Coast (Costa Mesa, California) College

George H. Pinckney, Jr., assistant football coach at Orange Coast College, has fielded football teams that averaged approximately 28 points a game while holding opponents under 7 points a game, on the average, over a four-year span. He has had a brilliant record on all levels of high school football—40 wins against 5 losses. His 1964-65 C teams at Huntington Beach High School went undefeated (16-0), winning two league titles. His last two seasons on the high school level were spent at Fountain Valley High School, where he compiled a record of 16-2 which included two league championships.

The California Interscholastic Federation classifies football players by age, height, and weight, to insure that boys will be competing on an equal physical basis.

Most schools have varsity, junior varsity, B, and C squads, with the C boys smallest, and the B players mostly freshmen and sophomores.

NOTE: I coach a B team in a school program that suits up 300 boys in the four classifications.

Only two coaches: The B coach has only one assistant and this comparative scarcity of coaches in today's highly specialized game makes two demands.

The head coach must be thoroughly organized by the time his season starts and the assistant must have acquired a keen sense of handling the boys according to plan.

NOTE: There are about 45 boys on a squad and two coaches would soon get into difficulty handling such numbers if they became inefficient.

No spring practice: Without the benefit of spring practice, the B coaches must move swiftly in selecting a team, because there are only 15 days of practice before the opening game.

The large number of raw candidates is another handicap, and it is imperative to devise a means of selecting the 11 best boys as quickly as possible.

NOTE: We have physical fitness records from the elementary schools that feed our system in the high school, and we have talks with the instructors who taught the boys who come to our team. However, this affords only a sketchy, preliminary idea of a new boy, but nothing on which to base selection or rejection.

Short-cut drills: To identify boys who will hit hard and show desire, we have devised two drills that have proven a short-cut in permitting us to name our finest prospects in a very short time.

I believe that one drill in particular, the Machine Gun Drill, makes a fast identification of a boy with football ability.

Machine gun drill: This play calls for a team of four players, who are set against one defensive player, or prospect. The team members are numbered 1-2-3-4, with No. 4 the ball carrier (Diagram 1).

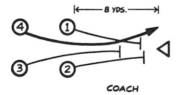

Diagram 1

As the coach calls each number, that player attempts to block out the defender and let the ball carrier through. The defender, therefore, must shed three blockers in order to tackle No. 4.

> NOTE: The boys who can withstand this stiff test obviously have courage and potential and are retained. As the boys become more proficient, the coach may speed up the cadence of the drill.

Touchdown drill: The other drill used extensively in the early season to pick out the best players is called the Touchdown Drill, and also is highly competitive.

This drill is staged in a rectangular area of 20 by 15 yards, with dummies, scrimmage vests, or other markers at the corners. One of the 15-yard long lines is called the goal line.

Two lines of defensive players line up behind the goal line, and two files at the other end, one file designated blockers and the other ball carriers. (See Diagram 2.)

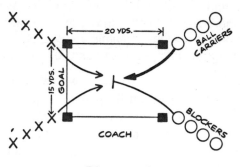

Diagram 2

NOTE: We give the linemen a chance as backfield men
to let them find out what it is like to carry the ball. This
habit also encourages enthusiasm.

Two-against-two: On the whistle, the ball carrier and his blocker
enter the area and try to score by crossing the goal line. The two
defenders also enter the area to prevent a score.

As a competition we usually play two out of three games, with the
winners of each game required to score 15 points, with 3 for a touchdown and 1 for a defensive save.

NOTE: The losers usually are asked to pay some sort
of penalty, such as push-ups, extra sprints, or a lap or
two.

This drill, like the Machine Gun Drill, not only will mark the
aggressive boys, but demonstrates to the coaches the candidates who
can run with the ball, block, pursue, and tackle in the open field.

NOTE: When there are only two coaches, the two drills
are invaluable in appraising candidates in the shortest
possible time.

Into the offense: After we have some working idea of the type of
personnel available, we start right into offensive techniques, because
that is the more difficult phase. Defense, we feel, is easier to teach and
can be picked up later.

I believe coaches, as a rule, underestimate the ability of the athlete to learn and perform difficult skills. I believe, from my experi-

ence, that the young athlete can learn anything the coach wants to teach
him, if the coach is a good teacher.

> NOTE: To emphasize that belief, I start teaching plays
> run out of our most difficult offensive set, and inform the
> boys.

Start at top: I feel that if the squad can handle the play from this
set, which is top difficulty, then building the offense will be an easy
task, because learning will progress rapidly.

We break the squad into the backs, under one coach, and the
linemen, under the other coach. Then the backs are teamed up in units.

> NOTE: As the backfield units run through skeleton
> plays, I circulate around the groups to discuss and
> demonstrate technique.

Backfield style: I feel that offensive execution must be flawless
in the backfield, with a heavy emphasis on ball-handling and faking.
Each back must believe he has an important function when he is
carrying the ball or acting as a decoy.

Near the end of practice, we bring backs and linemen together
with the hope that everything will fall into place. Generally it does, and
by the end of the season we generally are running 15 different offensive sets and many more plays and series.

5

Organizational Tips and Drills

by Bill Wagoner

Head Football Coach
Apalachiocola (Florida) High School

Bill Wagoner has been coaching high school football for 23 years and has an overall record of 158-85-9. At Apalachiocola, he has guided his squads to four undefeated seasons and has won the conference championship nine times. In 1968, the school won the state crown with a 12-0 mark. In 1973, his squad posted a 10-1 mark and went to the state play-offs.

I have found that organization is one definite essential in developing a football program in a small high school. You have to organize your plans thoroughly, and then fit them to the abilities of the boys available to you.

> NOTE: The following ideas and techniques have proven successful for me at Apalachiocola High School, and may very well fit another's philosophy of coaching.

Physical education: I teach physical education and therefore have the opportunity to observe the boys in my classes as to potential football players. We also strive to decide where these boys will function best in the program. The first thing we look for is a prospective quarterback. In a small school, you pretty much build your team around the talents of your quarterback.

> DRILLS: Every day during the physical education periods, I have the boys do agility drills. They are invaluable in that they enable football players to improve in quickness and body control without our having to sacrifice practice time—which can then be devoted to game-condition drills.

Defensive philosophy: We select defensive players on the basis of two merits—first, a boy must be able to tackle; secondly, he must display agility and quickness of movement. When we find 11 boys who have these abilities, we place them in positions where they will be most valuable to the team. Usually, we try to fill the defensive positions in the following order: linebackers, defensive ends, defensive halfbacks, the nose man, the monster man, the safety man, and finally the tackles.

Unit drills: A portion of the time allocated for defensive work is used for what we call "unit drills." One unit comprising ends, linebackers, halfbacks, and the safety man works on covering drop-back passing and on following the offensive flow. Also, the players are shown how to cover any offensive formation which might be used against them—the result being that a boy should seldom be surprised by a formation that he has never encountered in previous games.

Another unit consisting of the defensive ends, tackles, linebackers, and the nose man drills against an offensive line and a quarterback. This modified offense runs, plays, and blocks while the defense concentrates on perfecting its plays. Such a drill is valuable because it enables us to determine whether the defensive players are reacting quickly enough and whether they are covering their assignments.

> NOTE: The drill provides additional advantages, since it allows the player to learn offensive blocking assignments—and because there are no backs except the quarterback, it minimizes injuries.

Offensive philosophy: About a third of our practice time is spent on offensive play. For offensive drill we separate the backs and the linemen. I work with the backfield and my assistant works with the linemen. During this time, we concentrate on four plays which are basic to our running game. While the boys are running these plays, we check for the following: stance; initial steps as they fire out on the snap count; whether they are looking straight ahead prior to the snap count.

When the backs and linemen have completed their drills as separate units, and when we are satisfied that they know the four basic plays, then both groups are brought together to run plays against a defensive line with linebackers. A defensive secondary is never used during this drill, since we believe that the elimination of defensive backs reduces the possibility of injuries.

Calisthenics: At the beginning of each practice session, the players loosen up with calisthenics. This represents neither an extensive nor intensive segment of our sessions, since it has been our experience that when boys exert themselves too much during this session they will not be 100% effective during the other drills.

Drill program: After calisthenics, we work on three drills which we consider essential for sound football—blocking drill; tackling drill; linebacker drill.

1. Blocking drill—The boys line up facing five dummies which are placed about 4 yards apart. A coach gives the snap count and each of the players is checked for correct stance, for firing out on the snap count, and for the effectiveness of his block. Two blocks with each hip and with each shoulder are required.

> TIP: When a player has completed a block, he holds the dummy while the next player blocks; therefore, the drill is continued in a rotational sequence until all players have performed the prescribed number of blocks.

2. Tackling drill—The players form two parallel lines for the tackling drill (Diagram 1). One boy carries the ball while a player from the opposite line tackles him. During this activity, stress is directed toward having the tackler aim his face guard at the football in an attempt to knock it loose. Each player is required to make two tackles with each shoulder.

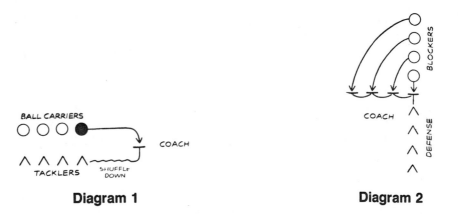

Diagram 1   **Diagram 2**

3. Linebacker drill—The backs, defensive ends, and linebackers are employed in the linebacker drill (Diagram 2). Four backs are aligned one behind the other with a defensive man facing them. The defensive player takes a linebacker stance with his feet squared up while a coach stands behind and uses hand signals to relay the snap count and direction to the offense. When the necessary signals are given, the backs fire out quickly in an attempt to block the defensive man.

> TIP: The player on defense must react instantly to the direction of flow, concentrate on playing the blockers off without giving ground, and prevent the blockers from reaching his feet and legs.

6

Factorizing Drills for Football Linemen

by Dr. Robert J. Brigham

**Chairman, Physical Education Department
and Athletic Director
Northern Illinois (Dekalb, Illinois) University**

Dr. Robert J. Brigham joined the coaching and teaching staff at Northern Illinois University in 1955, after a successful high school coaching career at Tuscola (Ill.) Community Schools. Besides coaching wrestling, Dr. Brigham heads the Physical Education Graduate Program and serves as athletic director.

Drills for football linemen must be scientifically based and specific to the objectives desired. The coach who thinks otherwise will receive less than maximum capacity from his charges.

> LAWS OF LEARNING: The very nature of football dictates that the coach observe the laws of learning —namely, learning is most effective when the student is motivated, the activity is geared to one's physical and mental ability, goals are apparent, and progress is indicated.

While obvious to the experienced coach, these very points are so often overlooked by the novice when developing his set of football drills.

Factorizing the drills: During the initial trial-and-error period of selecting and discarding football drills, we follow the concept of "factorizing" our drills. This simply means that our drills are designed to conform to the laws of learning and will develop specific physical factors, such as strength, agility, and speed.

> MOTIVATION: The key to our system of drills is motivation—defined for our purpose as self-rivalry. We encourage self-rivalry but subdue rivalry between athletes—which all too often causes resentment among players.

Drill program: The drills illustrated and described here deal with agility—the ability to change the direction of the body or parts of the body rapidly. This may involve small or large ranges of movement.

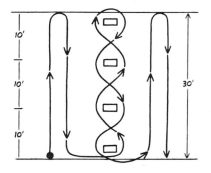

Diagram 1

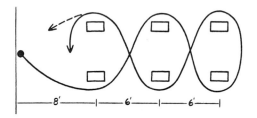

Diagram 2

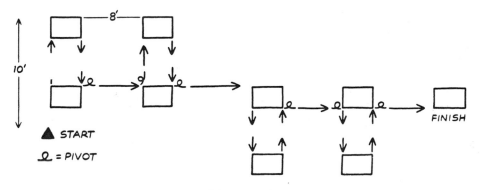

▲ START

♀ = PIVOT

Diagram 3

EMPHASIS: For agility in football, we emphasize (1) the ability to change directions, (2) reaction to pressures exerted, (3) coordination to eliminate mechanical errors, (4) good muscle rhythm.

Agility run: Diagram 1 illustrates our agility run. The starting position is the lineman stance. On the snap signal, the player runs 10 yards down the field and back—then he turns again and weaves through four dummies 10 feet apart. The runner then sprints 10 yards, turns, and sprints back to finish the drill.

OBJECTIVES: The agility run improves forward movement, right and left turns, and the ability to change directions rapidly.

Dodge run: For the dodge run the starting position is again the lineman stance. On the snap signal, the lineman runs around the dummies as shown in Diagram 2. Upon reaching the sixth dummy, the player repeats the circuit—and at the end of the second lap, sprints to the starting point.

OBJECTIVES: The dodge run improves the ability to change direction laterally while moving the body forward.

Shuttle run: The shuttle run, as illustrated in Diagram 3, is a combination of forward, backward, pivotal, and lateral movements. It's a good example of a meaningful drill, since such movements are necessary for good fundamental line play.

OBJECTIVES: The shuttle run perfects these basic movements as well as the coordination of the lineman executing them.

7

Drills for Eight-Man Football

by Dan Pero

Head Football Coach
Prospect (Oregon) High School

Dan Pero has been head football coach of eight-man football at Prospect High School for the last ten years. His overall mark is 65-15-2, and includes five league championships, two district championships, one state championship, and one state runner-up.

The backbone of any football operation is an organizational program for practice. The following method, with exact techniques intended to stress specific points, may serve as a guide for the new coach who is not in a position to read a dozen or more books on the eight-man game. There is a set pattern to the drills, and adjustments are made for it.

> EMPHASIS: The system is designed to stress the following points: (1) Agressiveness (physical-mental), (2) coordination, (3) physical fitness, (4) alertness, (5) discipline, (6) teamwork, (7) toughness, (8) quick reaction.

Competition featured: During the two weeks before school starts, we have an opening program with drills which last as long as five hours. As soon as school begins, every boy is required to participate daily for about two-and-a-half hours, with competition constantly emphasized. First practice is at 8 a.m. and the second at 4 p.m. on the field, with players ready to go. All run two to four laps before working on specialties for their positions. The coach's remarks should be brief and explicit, and should relate to the material in the notebook which is given to each player.

> NOTEBOOK: The notebook covers the chief rules; field regulations; dressing room requirements; injury prevention; diet; everyday fitness; calisthenics; and playbook material, such as formation, hole-numbering, pass and backfield patterns, play diagrams, signal calling and checking, and the defense routine.

Calisthenics drill: Each exercise is repeated 20 times, with that figure decreasing as the season progresses (Diagram 1). Most familiar maneuvers are side straddle hops (jumping jacks), sit-ups (hands on face bar, legs straight), cradle, push-ups (ten on hands, ten on fingers), bicycle (knees hitting shoulder pads), hops (20 in each direction), and ankle walk.

5 YARDS APART IN ALL DIRECTIONS

X X X X X X X X X X

X X X X X X X X X X X

X   X   X   X

LEADERS ARE SENIORS AND CO-CAPTAINS

Diagram 1

ENDURANCE: To develop endurance, run in position. On command, fall on stomach, get up fast, and run in place. On command, fall backwards, get up fast, and run in place.

There are many more recommended drills. For rotation of trunk, count four forward, four to right, four backwards, four to left, then decrease to three counts, two, and finally one, with hands on hips. For opposite toe touch, stand upright, touch right hand to left toe, contract shoulders, touch left hand to right toe, contract shoulders. For knee bends, touch toes, balance forward on toes to deep knee bends, bend back to touch toes, stand.

TREADMILL: Bend over on all fours for the treadmill, right leg up under the body. Next, switch legs so that left is under body and right foot is extended to the rear. Allow four counts for each repetition.

Three more: To execute arm throw from upright position, bend forward to touch toes; hit stomach with fist on way up; throw arms above head; hit stomach on way down. In leg stretch, extend left leg; put right leg underneath but towards outside; lean back and touch knee to ground; lean forward and touch head to left knee. In squat thrust, bend forward until hands are on ground, both legs underneath; extend both legs backward; return to starting position and stand.

AGILITY DRILLS: Divide into three lines and generally separate backs and linemen. The quarter eagle opens with feet apart at width of shoulders, heels flat on ground, and buttocks parallel to ground. Drill requires quarter turns right and left, for balance.

Wave drill: The four-point drill with football has men moving on all fours towards ball. On signal, men change direction. This is good for reactions and agility as well as endurance. At end, ball is held high for players to scramble forward and up to their feet to block pass. Players also yell "Beat (name of next rival)." The upright wave drill has players running in direction of football, and changing direction a number of times, with high leg action.

CONTACT: After turning a somersault, man assumes hitting position as soon as possible, hitting with either right or left forearm. In shoulder roll, throw right arm when going down on shoulder, cross to left hip, and on to feet in hitting position. After perfecting somersault and shoulder roll, players pair off to hit shoulders for contact.

The tiger roll or figure-eight starts with three players on all fours. Middle man rolls towards one of outside players, who in turn jumps over middle man and is about to roll under third player as he lands. It is good reactions and endurance drill.

Backs and ends: In balance drills for backs and ends, men run hard, touch ground twice consecutively with left hand, then same with right hand. Also, run hard, place left hand on ground and run around it, return to line with high leg action. Also, run in place with knees high, move forward on command with high-step gait, kick legs up high for another 5 yards, running at all times.

ANGLE AND TIRES: Run straight 5 yards and turn at 90-degree angle and sprint 7 yards (Diagrams 2 and 3) with tail down, legs high. In tires (Diagram 4) run with left foot into left row and right foot into right row. In tires with cross-over step (Diagram 5) hit each tire, but with opposite foot—left foot into right row and vice versa.

Spin and dive: For spinning drill on sleeves, start at left side, run and hit sleeve with right shoulder, spin into middle sleeve, spin and hit outside sleeve, and spin (Diagram 6). Set up in other line to go back

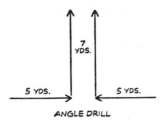

7
YDS.

5 YDS.   5 YDS.

ANGLE DRILL

Diagram 2

Diagram 3

Diagram 4

Diagram 5

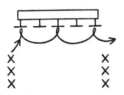

Diagram 6

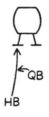

QB

HB

Diagram 7

COACH

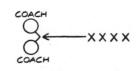

X X X X

COACH

Diagram 8

(T-43)

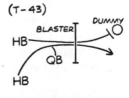

Diagram 9

with left shoulder. To develop right habits in halfback, practice dive drill (Diagram 7) into sled with low posture, head up, leg action. On handoff from quarterback, runner hits two-man sled with right shoulder to left side of sled and then repeats with left shoulder to right side, using either power drive or spin.

FOOTWORK: 1. Run at tackler or dummy, plant left foot; straight-arm, and hop away. 2. Run at tackler or dummy, plant right foot, kick foot across as stiff arm is given to change direction. 3. Run at air dummy and at contact throw arm on side of opponent through opponent's arms. This will aid in breaking tackle.

Bell dummies: Two bell dummies are held, base on ground. Dummies are pushed into ball carrier as he runs at them. Carrier must keep legs high, ball tucked in tight, and have speed and power. As he falls, his hand goes out for balance and extra yardage. Dummies should be pushed at knees, ankles, or squeezed together, to force a wide, high step (Diagram 8).

Guards, centers: There are a variety of drills for straight-ahead blockers and pulling guards on blaster, bell dummies, two-man sled, such as the cross-body, shoulder, belly slammer, drive-and-roll, with emphasis always on hitting impact.

TACKLING: On two-man sled, single line assembles to tackle, with players holding low carriage with head up, arms wide, and legs driving. Chatter step and alternate shoulders. In double line, two players tackle at a time to stress teamwork.

On tackling machine, player keeps balance to go either way against moving object. When tackling, helmet is used at center point, then it slides to one side for good shoulder contact. Dummy is driven hard with good lift to end of cable or weight. With two lines tackling, there is competition to hit first.

FORMATIONS: Backs and half of center contingent go to blaster; linemen to five-man sled. Backs run through blaster on play formations with blocking on dummy (Diagrams 9, 10). Entire line offense is run off against the sled (Diagram 11).

Secondary drills: While passers and receivers run through patterns, the defensive secondary goes through a varied drill. 1.

(I-68)

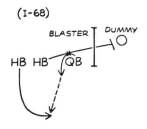

Diagram 10

Diagram 11

Diagram 12

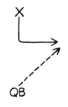

Diagram 13

Diagram 14

Diagram 15

Linebacker backpedals, guarding oncoming end until latter touches him (Diagram 12). 2. Linebacker goes with direction of fake using cross-over step (Diagram 13). 3. Secondary comes forward to catch pass (Diagram 14) or cuts to intercept oblique pass (Diagram 15).

> TOUGH PLAY: Two ends go down-field, about 10 yards apart, with defenseman between them. Quarterback fakes to one, passes to other (Diagram 16). Defenseman, fading with ends, must cut sharply to overhaul receiver.

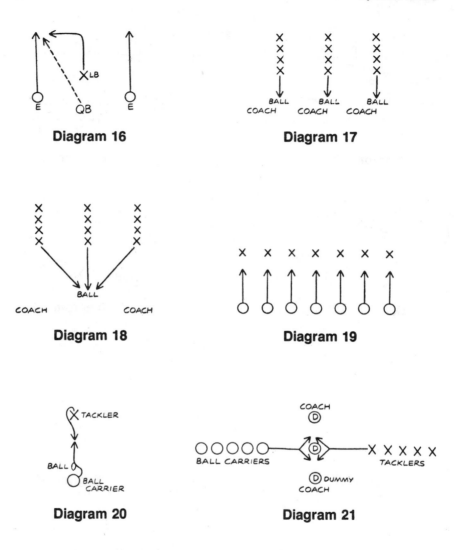

Diagram 16

Diagram 17

Diagram 18

Diagram 19

Diagram 20

Diagram 21

Fumble drill: Coaches work together, each with part of squad, in same area (Diagram 17). Players go slowly at first to master proper form to recover fumble. Player slides in after ball, pulling ball into stomach and doubling knees up around ball, while on side. Speed up, and in two days go into two lines, and then three, for competition to recover ball (Diagram 18). Coach throws ball to different points, to keep players on alert and on toes.

Diagram 22   **Diagram 23**

TACKLING FORM: 1. Start ball carrier at a walk towards tackler at beginning of season, to acquire correct
tackling procedure (Diagram 19). 2. Player lies on back
with ball behind other player, facing out. On snap count
player turns, picks up ball, and tries to elude tackle by
other player rolling off his back. Carrier is allowed only
one step on either side of tackler (Diagram 20).

Live tackling: Coaches support two outside dummies, with third
dummy in line in center. Carrier is on one side of middle dummy;
tackler lines up on other. Carrier runs to either side of center dummy; if
tackle is missed, tackler repeats until successful (Diagram 21). Also,
employ angle tackling to either side (Diagram 22). Double up two
tacklers on each carrier (Diagram 23).

SCRIMMAGE: Following the drill, squad is divided for
scrimmage, with equal time for all players, and equal
time for each squad on offense and defense.

Closing routine: To round out drill, one of three routines may be
picked on each day. One is the fireman's carry for 200 yards, another
the gauntlet, with every player taking a turn running the line, and the
third a series of 50- or 100-yard sprints.

8

"Concealed Running" Drills

by Bob Oravitz

Head Football Coach
North Schuylkill (Ashland, Pennsylvania)
High School

Bob Oravitz, head football coach at North Schuylkill High School, has an overall coaching record of 71-45-5. He has produced five straight championship teams at Mt. Carmel (Pa.) Catholic High School and Lourdes Regional (Shamokin, Pa.) High School. He is recognized as one of the foremost teachers of the art of placekicking. He has conducted football clinics at East Stroudsburg, Pennsylvania and Washington, D.C., plus one at Fort Meade, Maryland, for the Department of the Army.

Most boys grumble whenever they hear the coach shout, "Take five laps." They look at this running as drudgery—and it may even cut down on morale.

> AGILITY TIME: In place of this continuous running, we have substituted what I call "agility time." It's a period of 20 solid minutes of running (concealed in drills) following 10 minutes of calisthenics.

We have cut out most of our running of laps except for one lap around the track prior to football practice as a warm-up.

Procedure: Our agility time works in this manner:

1. We set up four separate areas or stations.

2. Coaches are divided among three groups—ends, backs, and interior linemen.

3. The coach of these positions rotates from station to station with his group. This allows the coach to become thoroughly acquainted with his group.

4. Once I blow the whistle to start the agility time, there is no stopping until the 20 minutes are completed.

> NOTE: I blow the whistle every 5 minutes for the groups to exchange stations. They run to the next station with their coach and get right into the next drill.

Our four stations are set up as follows:

Tire drill: (Figure 1.) We run through tires in three ways:

(a) The boys hit every tire with the side of their leg.

Figure 1

(b) They employ the cross-over step through the tires.

(c) They run on the tires. This is good for balance and control.

Weave and hurdle drill: (Figure 2.) Boys weave through maze (pegs in the ground) and hurdle dummies standing in between the pegs.

Figure 2

Plank drill: (Figure 3.) We perform this plank drill in three different ways:

(a) Boys travel down the plank with short, choppy steps and then roll over man stationed at the end of the plank on his fours.

(b) Boys use cross-over step down the plank and hurdle man at the end of the plank. This is good for body balance.

(c) Boys crawl on all fours while straddling plank.

Chalk line drill: (Figure 4.) We perform the chalk line drill in two ways:

(a) On call by the coach, the boys alternately hop on one leg, or

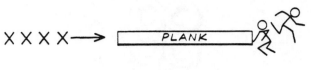

Figure 3

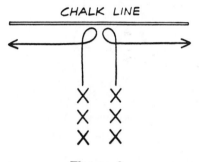

Figure 4

both legs, until they reach the chalk line. They then pivot and continue to the end of the chalk line.

(b) Boys spin to the right or left while running at medium speed on call of the coach. When they hit the chalk line they spin and continue to the end of the chalk line.

> SUMMARY: We believe in these drills. The boys are running—yet it is not a grind because of the variety of the program. After the agility time, we usually run 10- and 20-yard sprints.

9

Crowther Sled Blocking Drills

by Jerry Long

Assistant Football Coach
University of California, Los Angeles

Jerry Long has been in the football coaching ranks for 22 years. He handles the defensive interior linemen for the Bruins. Jerry joined Tommy Prothro's staff at Oregon State in 1961, where he served as a line coach before moving to UCLA in 1965. Prior to returning to his alma mater, Long served as the top aide and line coach at Willamette (Salem, Ore.) University for six years.

We teach most of the basic types of offensive blocks used today—one-on-one, post lead, trap blocking, crab blocking, and various forms of pass protection blocking. We can't discuss all of these techniques, but we can cover the teaching of the fundamentals of blocking on the crowther sled. This is one of the keys to the success we have enjoyed in this area.

> NOTE: Our football is based on the science of body mechanics. We begin by telling our players that offensively and defensively they must move toward their target on a low plane, strike through it, and finish by working their feet up underneath them with quick, choppy steps. We want their legs to bend and become a powerful coil and their backs to be straight as a ramrod. The head is up as it directs the force of the body. Where the head goes, the body follows.

When we begin the crowther drills, our theory is to break the blocking down into its simplest components in chronological order, perfect the detail of each part, and finally put them all together to form the whole block.

1. Triangle: Our players form a triangle with their arm and shoulder. As the player lifts his arm hand to his side, we have him bend his elbow. As he bends the elbow, his fist locates below his chin. With arm and shoulder, we want to lead with this triangle, shocking with it and providing a large blocking surface. The arm from the elbow to the shoulder should move straight up parallel to the body and legs.

2. Uncoil and extend through: Next, we teach the player to uncoil. Assuming we're going to block the crowther with the right shoulder, we place the boy at about an arm's length from the machine, shading the outside of the pad—with his left foot directly underneath him. His right knee will be touching the ground about even with the instep of the left foot. When he's in this position, the angle of his left leg will be at approximately 45 degrees. Assuming the man's head is up, his back will be at the same angle.

From this position, we want the player to roll his shoulder over the ball of the left foot, and at the same time drive off the left leg. If he keeps his head up, his force must go up through the the machine at approximately a 45-degree angle. The inside leg will come up naturally to the crowther pad. His left foot stays in place. On this drill, we just hit and hold.

> COACHING POINT: As the player holds next to the pad, the coach corrects the boy's angle, force, head, position, etc. What we are trying to emphasize here is that the foot you are driving from must be underneath you. If you roll your shoulder over the foot and your head is up, your force has to come up through the target in approximately a 45-degree angle.

A common fault here is that players have a tendency to over-stride. If the foot they are driving from is too far forward, the leg will be straight up and down. If they try to drive off the leg at that angle, their force comes straight up. Obviously, you can't get much force through your target doing this. Another fault occurs when the blocker's force stops as it reaches the pad. We want the force to go through the pad a couple of feet—so the hips must follow through to get the shock and follow-through we insist upon.

3. Step, one knee, and extend through: In all our blocking, we attempt to block up through an opponent. This drill gets us moving into the pad. Assuming we are blocking with the right shoulder, we place our players into a football position—tail down, head up, toes forward, feet about width of shoulders, arms hanging normally to the side. We take a short step with the left foot, making sure we won't over-stride, and at almost the same time touch the right knee to the ground next to the instep of the left foot—and drive through our target at about a 45-degree angle.

> NOTE: As the inside knee touches the ground, it comes up naturally to the crowther pad. As we make

contact striking through the pad, we hold against the
pad. As we strike through the machine, the machine
will bounce forward. It's very important that the head
remain up. Touching the ground with the inside knee is
an overemphasis of getting low, to come up through
the target.

4. Step, one knee, extend through, work feet: We repeat the
preceding drill—only now work our feet up under us and don't try to
move the machine back. We still want to strike through the pad, but
now we are emphasizing foot action.

TIP: Never take elongated steps. They should be short,
choppy, and digging steps.

It is very important that the feet be underneath the blocker. Our
inexperienced players' feet usually trail behind. If your feet trail behind, you have very little leverage on the man you are blocking.

TIP: We also pump the free arm—the arm that is not on
the machine.

5. Step, one knee, extend through, work feet, move machine:
We repeat the preceding drill, only now we are working our feet
moving the machine back.

6. Block the crowther, full speed: The last thing we do is block
the crowther full speed. We don't touch the inside knee now. We put
all these blocking techniques together. We like to think that we do
these things in chain reaction.

NOTE: We at UCLA believe that if a solid conditioning
foundation is built in a player, plus sound fundamental
techniques taught to him, you'll have a successful football player and team.

10

Windsprint Drills

by Stan Peters

Assistant Football Coach
Laney (Oakland, California) College

Stan Peters has been coaching high school and college football since 1963. In 1963, he was hired to rebuild the football program at Salesian (Richmond, Calif.) High School and lost little time. That year he posted a 6-3 mark (it was 2-7 in 1962); the next year, 1964, he compiled an 8-0-1 mark and won the league championship. From there he took his know-how to college ball and is presently assistant football coach at Laney College

We strongly believe that a well-conditioned football team must run; there should never be a time during practice when players are standing around. Even though our practice sessions are planned to keep all boys on the move, we still schedule extra running at the conclusion of practice. In this extra running, we apply our "diversity in windsprints" theory.

> RUNNING WITH A DIFFERENCE: While all coaches use some form of windsprints at the conclusion of practice, all too many use the same old type day after day—thus hampering 100% output by the squad. At Salesian High School, we use five different types of windsprints to get our players in top physical condition. They help obtain the desired results while presenting a varied approach to the task of conditioning by running.

15-yard sprint: In this excellent conditioning drill, we divide the team into two groups with one coach for each group. (All drills use two coaches, one with each team.) Each coach divides his group into three smaller groups of equal numbers and places them on the 15-yard line at each end of the field (Diagram 1). When the coach blows the whistle, one group runs down 15 yards and touches the goal line and turns around and runs back to the starting spot. Running down and back counts two trips; they continue running down and back 15 times until the coach blows the whistle. Then the next group takes off and follows the same procedure.

> NOTE: Each coach can run his groups as many times as needed, since two groups are resting while one is

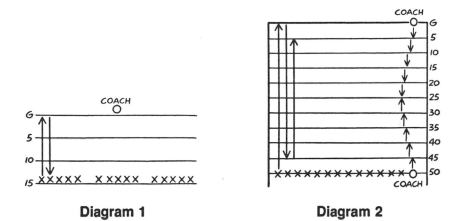

Diagram 1   **Diagram 2**

running. Each turn accounts for 225 yards of running. In this windsprint, the boys are thinking about the number of times they have to run rather than the distance.

The closer, the faster: This windsprint has an excellent psychological twist to it. We line up all the boys on the 50-yard line with one coach, while the other coach lines up on the goal line (Diagram 2). We have the boys sprint, by position, down to the other coach. After all the boys have completed this first run, the coach on the 50-yard line moves up 5 yards to the 45-yard line. The boys see the coach move up and they run harder now because it's a shorter distance. After the coach on the goal line sends all the boys back, by position, he moves up 5 yards. This continues until the coaches end up 5 yards apart.

> TWIST: We find that our players will run harder as the distance becomes shorter. In all, they run the course ten times for a total distance of 275 yards.

100-yard relay: Our third variation is a 100-yard relay in which we demand a maximum effort from all boys. We divide the group into four teams with equal numbers, and we try to pick teams having equal speed. Each group has one-half of the team on one goal line and an equal number on the other goal line (Diagram 3). Each player sprints 100 yards carrying a football, and must hand off behind the goal line to

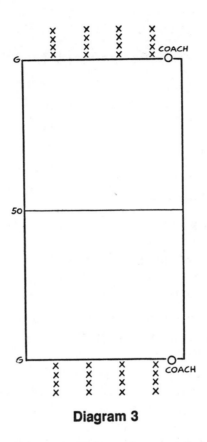

Diagram 3

the next member of his team. This continues until the relay is complete
and the first, second, third, and fourth places are determined.

One coach is on the goal line to watch the hand-offs and to start
and determine the winners of the relays. We run five relays, and the
team that wins is finished with this phase. The second-place team must
run one lap; the third-place team two laps; the fourth-place team three
laps. To add interest, we give each team a 5-yard lead inverse to their
finishing position. The fourth-place team gets a 15-yard lead; the
third-place team 10 yards; the second-place team 5 yards.

> 100% OUTPUT: Our boys give 100% because they
> want to beat the three teams they are running
> against—and becuase they want to show how fast they
> are.

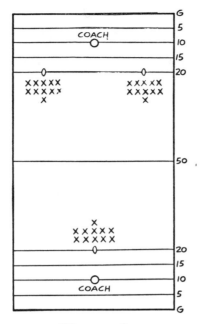

Diagram 4

20 plays in 15 minutes: Our 20 plays in 15 minutes is an excellent drill to check both physical and mental reactions under pressure, as well as being a physical conditioner. One coach takes the first offensive team to one end of the field, and the other coach takes the second and third offensive teams to the opposite end of the field (Diagram 4).

Each team will start with the ball on the 20-yard line, huddle, and run a play with perfect execution. Every member of that team must run down-field 10 yards, behind the coach, and run back and huddle up on the 19-yard line. They will follow the same procedure again and huddle up next on the 18-yard line, and so on. Each team will have 15 minutes to execute 20 perfect plays. If a play is broken—a missed assignment, fumble, pass dropped, or if any member fails to run 10 yards—they must run the play over from the same yard line. For every play under 20 that they do not run in 15 minutes, they must run one lap after practice.

PRESSURE TO PERFORM: In the last 2 or 3 minutes, when the team is down to the 4- or 5-yard line, they

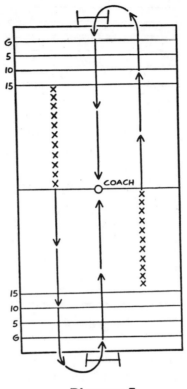

Diagram 5

should run the goal-line offense. There is great pressure to perform even though the boys are tired and time is running out. In this drill, they are running a minimum of 400 yards in 15 minutes; later, you can cut the time to 12 and then 10 minutes.

Follow the leader: Here we divide the squad into defensive and offensive teams, or by backs and linemen, and sometimes by positions. We tell the leaders where to run and they take off at half speed. They will run from one spot, and back to the coach, and then off again to another spot. As an example, in Diagram 5, we would tell them to run around one goal post and then around another—or any other landmark. We keep them running as long as we feel it's necessary.

This is a good drill for various reasons: We use different leaders, such as a third-string guard or any other boy who doesn't play much; it helps to make the reserves feel important. You can put a loafer in front and he has to hustle or else get run over. By keeping in close order, the boys can get the feeling of unity; we have them chant "Go-Go" while they are running.

> COACHING POINTS: We vary these five windsprints throughout the week, and normally use two or three of these drills in one practice. It depends on how much running and conditioning we feel we need. The psychological approach is extremely important in windsprints—only through varying your program can you obtain the maximum effort out of running. It has worked that way for us.

11

All-Purpose Helmet Drill

by Billy O'Brien

Head Football Coach
Great Bridge (Chesapeake, Virginia) High School

Billy O'Brien has just completed his 19th year of coaching football at Great Bridge High School. His overall record to date is most impressive—141 wins, 40 losses, and 10 ties.

Our helmet drill lets one coach teach about 15 to 20 players (backs and ends) how to run with the football. All we need is four helmets, a football, and the players. The incidence of injury in the drill is virtually nil.

The main objective of this drill is to teach the players to spin, to place the ball from one hand to the other, to cross over and fade away, and to run both a single and double fake. The drill teaches all of them from the same placement of the helmets on the ground. In addition, it is good for promoting agility and quickness.

The helmets are laid out as in Diagram 1, which also shows the spin drill. In the spin, the boys run at the helmets and spin at each one, keeping both hands on the ball. The chief coaching point on the spin is to insist that the boys keep the knees high. This is important, not only for breaking away from a tackler, but also for preventing sprained ankles if cleats get caught in the turf. The ball must be carried with both hands over the end and arms enclosing it.

After completing the spinning before each helmet, the player carries the ball to the waiting line of players and hands off to the first one in line, who then runs the drill himself.

In the cutting drill (Diagram 2), the players cut around the helmets while changing the ball from one hand to the other on each cut. The main coaching point here is the proper roll from side to side and a tight hold after each change. This must become a conditioned reflex on the part of the player, and must be done properly if fumbles are to be avoided. It is imperative that the ball be pressed and carried tightly

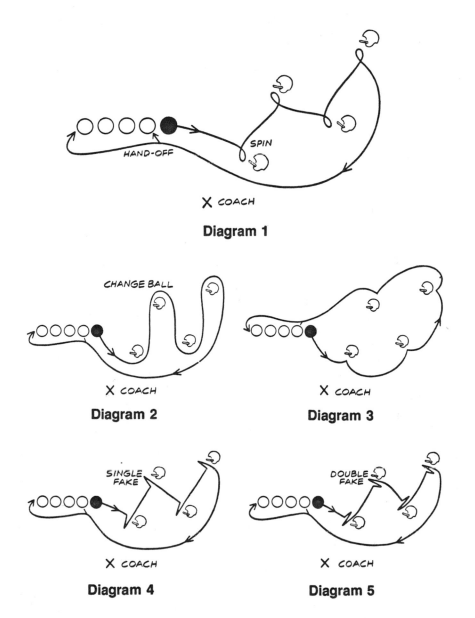

HAND-OFF

SPIN

X COACH

Diagram 1

CHANGE BALL

X COACH

Diagram 2

X COACH

Diagram 3

SINGLE FAKE

X COACH

Diagram 4

DOUBLE FAKE

X COACH

Diagram 5

after each exchange, in either the left hand and arm or right hand and arm.

The cross-over and fade-away (Diagram 3) is done in a clockwise, then counter-clockwise, direction, so that a left leg cross-over and then a right leg cross-over, can be drilled. At each helmet, the stiff-arm can be simulated. It is important that at least a two-step fade-away be used at each helmet.

In the fakes (Diagrams 4 and 5), both the single and the double, the chief coaching point is to make sure that the player's head and trunk is moved in the direction of the fake.

I feel that the most important thing in coaching is the development of the conditioned reflex, so that the boys will do the right thing *automatically* under game conditions. My experience is that the running maneuvers from our helmet drill become conditioned reflexes.

> NOTE: You can keep up enthusiasm for this drill by setting up two groups of helmets, dividing the players into two groups, and running the drill as a relay. Another method: Use a stopwatch and time each runner competitively.

For a faster drill: You can have a number of the boys with footballs in their hands, and one starts as soon as the man ahead of him makes the first or second, spin or cut or fake by the helmets. The handoff is to the first man in the line *without* a football at the end of the drill.

12

Challenge Hamburger Drill

by Bob Collison

Head Football Coach and Athletic Director
Richfield (Minnesota) High School

Bob Collison's ten-year record as head football coach at Richfield High School is 59 wins, 19 losses, and 3 ties. This includes three league championships—1961, 1963, and 1967, and one state championship—1963. In 1969, he became Athletic Director at Richfield High School and currently holds that position.

I have always felt our "hamburger" drill (Diagram 1) an essential in building winning players. The problem: As our squads got larger, it took too much time.

> HAMBURGER DRILL: Place two dummies 3 yards apart. Put a defensive man opposite an offensive man and a back 4 yards from the line of scrimmage. The coach stands by one dummy and flips the ball to the back on the starting count. Each man is given three tries on offense and three tries on defense. The winner is determined by the gains made by the back. If he gains more than 3 yards, the offense is awarded a point; if he makes less than 3, the defense scores a point. The ball carrier must run on the side the blocker puts his helmet. The boys and/or coaches determine the winners.

By adding a challenge and prestige feature to the drill, we have done these two things:

1. The boys work harder at the drill than ever before, thus improving its effectiveness.
2. They work the drill before the formal practice session, thus giving the staff that much more time for other things.

Challenge: On a 4' x 6' piece of plywood painted with the school colors, we arrange six rows of 12 hangers (cup hooks). We use a plain 2" metal-rimmed tag for each player's name (the 12th tag is for injured

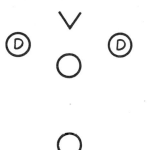

Diagram 1

players or the occasional alternate used on a team). From this, we can visually show a daily listing of our teams.

A player is allowed to challenge the man in the position directly above him in a hamburger drill. Arrangements are made at the beginning of practice by notifying the coaches and opponent. The winning boy (see description of drill on preceding page) is responsible for making the change on the team board. (The coaches also make changes in team position when a player becomes more proficient than the man above him.)

> NOTE: The ball carrier is picked from third- and fourth-team backs. They are neutral, and the work is fun, so there is no problem in finding willing volunteers.

Prestige: When our squads got larger, we turned a small auxiliary locker room into a ''varsity'' locker room, with a sign over the door reading: ''Through This Door Pass the Toughest Football Players in the Lake Conference.'' We started by putting the two co-captains in the room, and added to it any boy who could stay with either of them in a challenge hamburger drill.

> PRIDE: The coaches and captains originally made the decision on who was in the room. Pride in accomplishment is now so strong that it is almost entirely left up to the boys in the room.

To get into the room, a boy may challenge out of position; i.e., a 160-pound back may challenge a 200-pound lineman. (In a challenge of this type, the back is considered a blocker working directly on a lineman, as in the situation where a lineman attempts to block a linebacker.)

I find these results—all beneficial—have come about:

1. The challenges are consistently tougher than regular practice. Each effort is 100%, with no opportunity to pair up and take turns making each other look good.

2. Morale is improved. No one complains that he doesn't have a chance.

3. The boys now work on weak points automatically when they show up early for practice.

4. In out-of-position challenges, the poorest boys in the varsity room are usually the ones challenged; therefore, they get the most work and make the most progress.

I feel that this combination of challenge and prestige has been a great developer of mental toughness and morale, in addition to the improvement in skill the drill brings, and has contributed much to our success.

13

The "Dutch Mill" Drill

by Ray Cliffe

Head Football Coach
Cleveland (St. Louis, Missouri) High School

Ray Cliffe's record as head football coach at Cleveland High School is 102-65-12 in the tough St. Louis Public High School League (ten teams). His record includes two undefeated teams (1965 and 1968) and a public high school championship in 1969.

We use our "Dutch Mill" drill to teach a second reaction to our offensive and defensive football personnel. It is ideally suited for guards, tackles, and ends.

TIP: We recommend that the drill be run by separate groups of all line positions at the same time in three areas under the observation of a line coach.

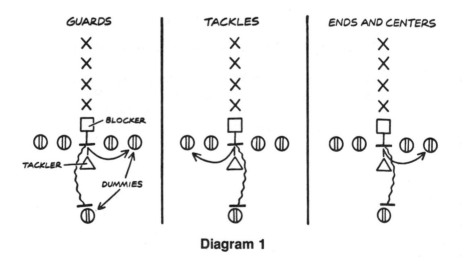

Diagram 1

The drill works this way: The offensive lineman blocks on the signal of the ball carrier (the next man in line) behind him. After making this primary block, the offensive blocker executes a down-field block on the dummy.

The defensive lineman hits with explosive leverage and closes the gap to tackle the ball carrier. After executing this move, he scrambles to tackle a dummy either to the left or right of the blocking area. The left or right signal is given by the coach.

This is a rotating drill: (1) The ball carrier becomes the next offensive blocker; (2) the defensive tackler becomes a ball carrier (going to the end of the line); and (3) the offensive blocker becomes the defensive man.

14

The "Canvas Line" Drill

by Art Hass

Athletic Director

Austin (Minnesota) High School

Art Hass' career record as a head football coach is 165 wins, 53 losses, and 8 ties. The 1969 season was his last as head coach at Austin High School. He is now athletic director at the same school.

Backfield practice is usually a boring time for linemen. All that they have to do is "sit in there" and give the backs a point of reference for hole numbers and so on. Not only does this bore linemen, it wastes their time—time that should be used for line practice. Any coach knows that even the best backfield cannot win games without solid line play.

THE PROBLEM: Linemen waste their time in backfield practice, but the backs need points of reference for line splits and hole numbers. The problem is, therefore, to give the backfield their reference points without wasting the linemen's time. Through the use of the "canvas" line, we have solved this problem.

Here is how it works (Figure 1):

We have a canvas 1 foot wide that has hole numbers and line splits painted on it. The length of the canvas depends, of course, on the type of line and the splits you use. The canvas is then spiked to the ground. In doing group work, all that the backs have to do is run over the number indicating the play. A reserve center is the *only* lineman needed.

RED VESTS: In some cases, we lay red scrimmage vests on the ground to indicate the location of the defensive backs. We feel this helps us when we run pass patterns.

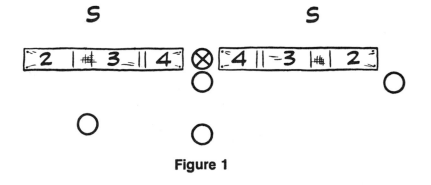

Figure 1

15

Fence-Post Drills

by Bill McArthur

Head Football Coach

Oregon College (Monmouth, Oregon) of Education

Bill McArthur is starting his 28th season as head football coach at Oregon College of Education. His overall record is 123-92-4 and includes eight conference titles and three co-titles. Bill McArthur was district Coach-of-the-Year (NAIA 1972) for all sports; Football and Golf Coach-of-the-Year (1972-73); and Northwest Coach-of-the-Year (1973).

We save a lot of time, and learn a lot of football, with a few simple wood posts. Here's how we do it: We sink a series of 4" x 4", 8-foot posts about 2½ feet in the ground (5½ feet above ground). One set consists of five posts (simulating an odd defensive alignment) and the other consists of six posts (for an even defensive alignment).

We use these posts in many ways:

1. *Running plays:* All of our boys do not report for practice simultaneously. The quarterbacks and centers report 5 minutes early. As the other boys come out, they jog a lap and report to the posts. We run through our plays with skeleton groups, filling in as the boys report.

> NOTE: If there are any new plays, I give them to the boys at the end of this 15-minute period, and we run through them against the posts.

2. *Ball handling drills:* The boys run through the posts as shown in Diagram 1, shifting the ball each time a post is passed.

3. *Agility drills:* Running the same pattern around the posts as shown in Diagram 1, we run these agility drills:

- We send them around the posts at flat speed.
- We send them out at 2-second intervals, so they must dodge fellow players coming back.
- We send them out at 2-second intervals, each with a ball, for quick footwork and dodging coming back.

Diagram 1

NOTE: We find these drills are excellent for the building of endurance.

4. *Low charging:* We put a low rope across the poles. We find it helps the backs stay low as they come through on their play assignments (Diagram 2).

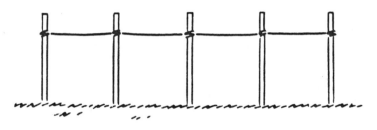

Diagram 2

5. *Hole identification:* Early in the season, with our freshmen, we place cards on the ropes to help the men visually identify our hole numbering system (Diagram 3).

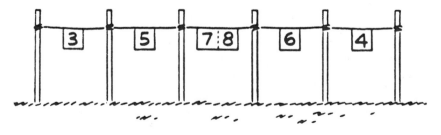

Diagram 3

Post Points

● With our blocking system, we find the younger boys in particular seem to run truer patterns by being on the posts.

● We can work the backs separately for speed and agility.

● When the linemen are on the posts, they do not block the posts, but go through them with the correct shoulder position and proper foot patterns. The trap men merely go by on the inside of the posts.

● We can run from either side of the posts, and move them if the ground gets chewed up.

● We have placed chalk circles on the ground to correctly space the newer men for depth and lateral spacing.

● We find the posts are a good rallying point, and provide a meaningful warmup period instead of just running or chasing after a football.

● Boys who have trouble learning assignments can be assigned to the posts with a graduate assistant while the senior members of the coaching staff work on their activities.

The posts give us a starting point for the efficient development of scrimmage activity. We start with the posts, then move to dummy scrimmage with air dummies, then to dummy scrimmage without dummies, and finally to live scrimmage.

16

The "Eyeball" Drill

by Tom Parry

Head Football Coach

Central Washington (Ellensburg, Washington) State College

Tom Parry is a 25-year coaching veteran at both the high school and college level. While at Wenatchee (Wash.) Junior College, his squads won and tied for the Washington State Junior College crown. At present, he is head football coach at Central Washington State College.

We use our "eyeball" drill for our linemen to encompass many of the fundamentals we wish to stress in our defense against the passing game. We think it keeps a maximum number of players active, lends itself to game conditions, and can be adjusted to simulate the next opponent's passing style.

> NOTE: We usually cover with seven men and rush with four. We instruct our rushers to look at the passer's eyes, feeling that eventually he will have to look at his target.

We set up as shown in Diagram 1, and the coach (or quarterback) takes the snap and works a pass to any of the set receivers. Note these features of the drill:

1. After the pass blockers have held their blocks for a required period of time, they go over and become pass receivers.
2. The pass rushers turn around and become pass protection blockers.
3. The receivers become rushers. (Rotation continues.)
4. Any defensive alignment can be used. (If your opponent rolls out, sprints out, or bootlegs, this can be incorporated by the passer.)
5. Both defense against the passing game and pass protection blocking are stressed in the drill.

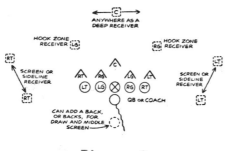

Diagram 1

We instruct our men as follows in looking at the passer's eyes:

- If he looks through you, push off from the pass blocker, raise your hands and arms, and force the passer to throw over you.
- If the passer looks down, it is usually the draw play, since he will be looking at the back who will carry the ball.
- If it is a screen to the flat, we will recognize it since we are staying with the pass blocker and he will leave to go to the flat.
- If it is a screen through the middle, we feel our hands high up will help obstruct it.

17

Up-to-Date Tire Drill

by Joseph F. Thomas

Athletic Director

Chaminade (Mineola, New York) High School

After 22 years as head football coach at Chaminade High School, Joseph F. Thomas retired from active coaching to devote full time to his duties as athletic director. His overall coaching record is 120 wins, 46 losses, and 7 ties and includes six Metropolitan Catholic High School league championships. Coach Thomas was elected President of the Metropolitan C.H.S.F.L. in 1968 and was re-elected in 1970.

Many of the fundamentals involved in the game of football are incorporated in this drill which has long been one of our favorites here at Chaminade. The old tire drill was used primarily for the development of high knee action. The objectives of our up-to-date version are many: (1) agility; (2) balance; (3) strengthening of the ankle and knee joints; (4) endurance; (5) correct blocking position; (6) correct defensive position; (7) sustained drive; and (8) desire and courage.

> BE CAREFUL: We use this drill practically every day in pre-season practice. We use it, however, *only as soon as we are ready for contact*. It is a rough, demanding drill and boys with a history of chronic knee or ankle injury may not be able to participate. We have checked the drill and definitely feel that it has aided us in keeping ankle and knee injuries at a minimum due to the gradual stretching of the joints that it provides.

We work the drill in two separate units: (1) interior linemen; and (2) backs and ends. The drill itself has three phases or variations, each a progression and a little more difficult than the preceding one. Here is how it works.

The tires are placed in position so that there are no holes available for the players to step into. This forces them to land on the tires themselves which, because of the unevenness, makes it difficult for them to maintain balance unless they stay in good football position with short, choppy steps and body kept low. Boys who run high have difficulty remaining on their feet and are frequently run over. Diagram

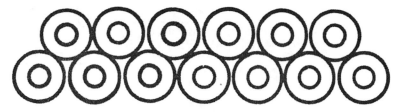

Diagram 1

Diagram 1a

1 shows how we arrange the first layer of tires and Diagram 1a shows how the lineup looks after we add the second layer.

Here are our three phases of the tire drill:

Phase 1: The players line up at one end of the tires as shown in Diagram 2. A captain is assigned to each group of five boys. Each group is then given a number which we keep throughout the season to save time. When we make up groups, we mix centers, guards, tackles and so on among interior linemen. Group # 1 in the diagram begins by holding heavy dummies at the opposite end of the tires. Group # 2 starts with a forward roll. The first man rolls to the right, the second to the left, and so on to avoid any pile-up. Each man runs through the tires and executes a good shoulder block on a dummy that hasn't been blocked. Group # 3 starts its roll as soon as the last man in Group # 2 has left the tires. Group # 2 takes Group # 1's place at the dummies and is under *immediate* pressure from Group # 3. Group # 1 goes to the end of the line. The men holding the dummies should be encouraged to maintain their position. The coach can have each group go through the tires as many times as he feels is necessary.

Phase 2: As I mentioned earlier, this is a progression of phase 1. It is run in exactly the same manner. The only difference is that the

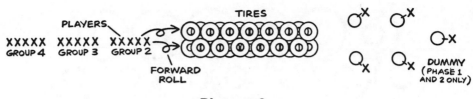

Diagram 2

men holding the dummies use light air dummies instead of the heavy ones, which makes the blocking part more difficult.

Phase 3: In this phase, no dummies are used. The boys are left on their own. This is the "tough" one, especially when the boys are told to hold their ground. It should only be used after the first two phases of the drill have been perfected.

Every one of the phases of the drill should be conducted with speed. The fundamentals of good blocking position and defensive stance should be stressed at all times. The first time the drill is run, it should be done slowly with concentration on correct execution. The boys should be encouraged to fight for good blocking position. When a boy knocks another dummy-holder down, we make a big thing of it so that everyone is trying to flatten someone else. Boys who are able to keep their position are lauded. This brings about a lot of competition.

18

The "Man-Maker" Drill

by Larry Markley

Head Football Coach

Haven (Kansas) High School

Larry Markley has been coaching high school football since 1960. He started at Marquette (Kan.) High School, where in two years his teams won the league championship both years and were undefeated and scored on only once. He is presently head football coach at Haven (Kan.) High School, where the past six years his teams have won 38 and lost 18, tying for the league championship and winning the district in 1971. His overall coaching mark is 72-49-4.

Time is always an important factor in scheduling high school football practice. Thus, effective and purposeful drills must be used. We use a multipurpose drill called the "man-maker" which has been very effective. Here's the way we do it:

Basic set-up: Diagram 1 illustrates the basic set-up for the drill. Since our basic defense is a 5-4, all of the following diagrams include a 5-4 defense. This drill is not, however, limited to a 5-4, but could be adapted to any defense.

Functions of the "Man-Maker"

- Keeps approximately 30 boys busy at one time (an important factor when working with a relatively small squad).
- Can be used for both defensive and offensive units.
- Heart of the offense is run against our basic 5-4 defense.
- Gives us an opportunity to use our best defensive tackles, ends, and corner linebackers against the best offensive personnel.
- Two offensive and defensive units are ready to alternate units after every five or six plays. Each boy on the alternate unit can watch his position and pick up any helpful hints or mistakes.
- Our coaches have an opportunity to correct any mistakes in play execution.
- Puts a heavy burden on the defenses, but it has paid big dividends.

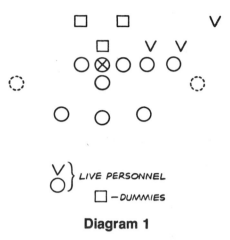

Diagram 1

Offensive Techniques

Power sweep outside and inside: (Diagrams 2 and 3.) Using down-blocking, the guards and backs take the first wrong-colored jersey that is standing. On the power sweep outside, we try to hook the immediate outside defenders and try to kick the end and cornerback out on the power sweep inside.

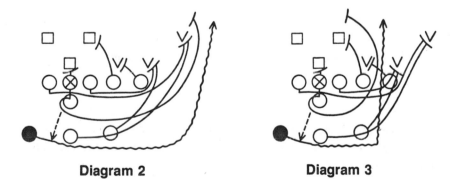

Diagram 2   **Diagram 3**

The fullback slant and option: (Diagrams 4 and 5.) A double team block is used in both cases to give the quarterback assurance of complete play execution as he slides down the line of scrimmage. An effort is made to put a tremendous amount of pressure on the defensive end in the hope that he will commit himself first.

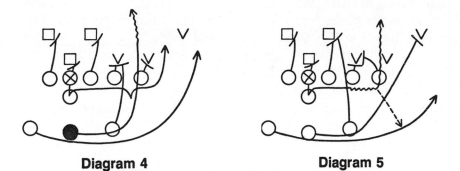

Diagram 4   **Diagram 5**

Roll-out run-pass option: (Diagram 6.) If the defense rushes quickly, the quarterback sets up and throws. If the defense floats, the quarterback is instructed to yell "go" and run with the ball.

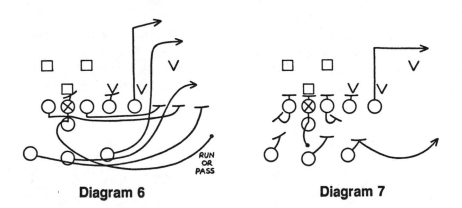

Diagram 6   **Diagram 7**

The drop-back pass: (Diagram 7.) The end emphasizes a 90-degree turn and looks for the ball on the second step past the corner. The right halfback will block for two counts and swing out as a safety valve.

Defensive Techniques

Tackle: The tackle plays on the outside shoulder of the offensive tackle. He will use a forearm shiver or lift and cover outside, either penetrating or sliding along the line of scrimmage. Since the tackle will be down-blocked or two-timed on all of our running plays, our tackles are instructed to fight pressure and/or roll out.

End: The defensive end plays on the outside shoulder of the offensive end with his inside foot forward. Our end should try to execute three maneuvers: (1) Always hit or push the offensive end, take two steps past the line of scrimmage, and box. By hitting the offensive end, this minimizes his effectiveness in down-blocking, double-teaming, or releasing for a pass reception. (2) Take out all of the interference possible. (3) Either make or be in on the tackle.

> NOTE: A game is played between our offensive guards and defensive ends. The guards are told to never leave a defensive end standing, and our defensive ends are told that they can never be knocked off their feet. This creates game condition competitiveness.

Corner linebackers: Corner linebacker coverage is, of course, dependent on field position. However, normally our corner backs play 2 yards back and 2 yards outside the defensive end against a straight-T. When a wing man is present to his side, he will play 3 yards outside and 1 yard back. When the wing is away, he plays 3 yards back and 1 yard outside. The cornerbacks are instructed to rush and put on the pressure against any power sweep or roll-out their way. Against the dropback pass he has flat coverage.

The "man-maker" drill puts considerable pressure on the defense. And, conversely, when the defense starts functioning correctly, the pressure is placed upon the offense. By putting our best defense against our best offense, a highly spirited practice session ensues. If boys can handle this situation in practice with proper execution, they will be poised, confident, and competitive during a ball game.

19

"Porta Pit" Tackling Drills

by Tom Richards

Defensive Coach

Loyola (Los Angeles, California) University

Tom Richards has been defensive coach at Loyola (Los Angeles, Calif.) University for the past seven years. Loyola has been among the top ten in defense in small colleges in California, four out of five years. Coach Richards received his B.A. from California State at Los Angeles and his M.A. from Pepperdine University.

At Loyola (Los Angeles, California) University, we have never had a player hurt in tackling practice. We are able to teach "full go" tackling with no worry of an injury because of our "Porta Pit Drills."

> NOTE: First, the porta pit can be used at any level of competition. It is excellent in preventing the development of "buck fever" among the young, inexperienced players. Using the porta pit enables a coach to allow his players to have solid contact during the week of a game, without the worry of losing a player due to possible injury.

Hit-and-Lift Technique

The method used for tackling at Loyola University is that of the "hit and lift" technique. However, teams using the spear type of tackling can also use the porta pit.

Coaching Point

One of the best ways to show players that falling into the pit will not affect them is to have one of the coaches run and then leap up in the air and fall into the porta pit.

This accomplishes two things:

1. Players relax and look forward to tackling into the pit.
2. It demonstrates that no matter what the age, anyone can jump into the porta pit at ground level and not get hurt.

Fall Drill

The first drill we use is the fall drill (Diagram 1). The players set up by standing at the sides of the porta pit, making four lines. One player in each line stands in front of the pit with his back to it and the tackler faces him. If the players are experienced (college or high school varsity), they just lock their arms on the player to be tackled and then they switch positions.

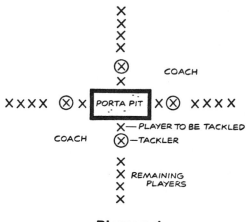

Diagram 1

NOTE: However, for the young, inexperienced player who has never been exposed to "contact," the player just falls into the pit backwards by himself—or the young player has his teammate hold onto him in a tackling position and both players fall into the pit together.

Hit-and-Lift Drill

On the command, "Rube," the tackler assumes a hitting position, placing his face mask on his teammate's belt buckle. Upon the command, "Hit," the tackler locks his hands and lifts the player up, "stutters" in place, and on the whistle the tackler drives his teammate into the porta pit.

COACHING POINT: Don't just let the players fall into the pit—have them drive hard through their man. To keep the drill moving, as one tackler is stuttering, the command of "Rube" is given for the next tackler.

On-the-Back Tackling

This drill has the player who is being tackled moving back and forth in front of the pit. At the same time, the tackler lays on the ground, 2 to 3 yards away (the tackler should not get more than 3 yards from the pit). The reason for the tackler being fairly close to the pit is that this eliminates a possible injury from being off-balance and not under control when he makes contact. Too much momentum by a player can cause both players to go over the porta pit and onto the ground.

On a command by the coach, usually a silent wave of the hand, the tackler moves quickly up off the ground and concentrates on the belt buckle of his teammate. Upon contact, the tackler performs the "hit and lift" tackling ritual. When the coach blows the whistle, the tackler takes the player into the porta pit.

NOTE: Once both players are in the pit, they should move out of it as quickly as possible. The fastest way is to have both players roll out to the sides of the pit. To facilitate time, as the two players have hit the pit, the next tackler should have been given the signal to participate in the tackling drill.

Side Tackling Drill

The players who are to be tackled line up to the side of the pit and the tacklers line up facing the front of the pit (Diagram 2).

On command, the player being tackled starts towards the pit. The tackler keeps his eyes on the belt buckle, with the emphasis on sticking the head in front and locking the arms around the thighs and driving through the player into the porta pit.

NOTE: The players rotate lines and sides of the pit. Backs should carry a ball on all tackling drills.

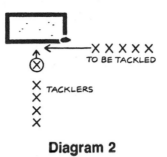

Diagram 2

Pass Receiver's Drill

This drill is for offensive players. The receiver stands to the side of the pit. Either a coach or a player throws the ball to the receiver as he runs in front of the pit. As the receiver catches the ball, a player tackles him as hard as possible. This drill will help receivers hold onto the football when being tackled (Diagram 3).

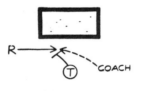

Diagram 3

Defensive Back Drill—
Go Through the Receiver

A receiver stands on the other side of the porta pit facing a coach or a passer. The defensive back stands behind the receiver, keeping a normal cushion.

As the ball is thrown to the receiver, the defensive back goes through and over the player to the ball. This drill teaches the receiver to hold onto the ball while being hit from behind. At the same time, the defensive back is learning how to play through the offensive receiver on a hook or curl pattern (Diagram 4).

Diagram 4

Goal-Line Leap Drill

Another drill that can be used for backs is the technique of a back vaulting over the defensive line on the goal line. Just place three defensive linemen in front of the pit, with three offensive linemen facing them, and allow a back to run up and leap over the defensive players into the pit. This simulates the goal-line score.

Conclusion

The use of the porta pit is a tremendous time saver to coaches. In 15 minutes, the entire defensive team can be put through the tackling drills. It is also a great morale booster and the players have fun doing the drills and utilizing the pit. One of our traditions is that after practice the entire defensive team carries the porta pit to the shed—and all the players chant, ''Do we love the porta pit? . . . Yes, we love the porta pit.'' This is morale.

20

Drills for Coaching the Punter

by Don Ault

Head Football Coach
Bethany (West Virginia) College

Don Ault was head football coach of Bellaire (O.) High School for eight years—and during his last five years there, he posted a record of 39-7-5. He was named Coach-of-the-Year twice and All-Star Coach twice. At present, he is head football coach at Bethany (W.Va.) College.

Most high school teams average four or five punts per game. If your punter averages 35 yards per kick, he will gain from 140 to 175 yards each game for his team. When we look at the kicking game from this standpoint, it's apparent that punting is one of the most potent offensive weapons.

> STUDY AND PRACTICE: Any phase of football that can gain 175 yards each game must be studied and practiced. No skill in football is natural. The right-handed player does not like to block with his left shoulder, lead with his left foot, or get down in a left-handed stance. But after being drilled in such a fashion, he'll often do a better job. Punting is much the same.

Find a boy with a good leg snap and great desire, who is willing to work during the spring and summer, and you have the prerequisite of a punter. Coach him in proper warm-up, stance, dropping of the football, meeting the ball, and follow-through—and you'll lead your league in punting yardage.

Weekly schedule: Here's our weekly punting schedule once the season is under way: Monday—Ten minutes during pre-practice specialty period. Use centers. Fifteen minutes of team punt cover and punt return; Tuesday—Eight minutes during pre-practice specialty period; Wednesday—Ten minutes during pre-practice specialty period. Three good punts after practice; Thursday—Ten punts before practice. Ten minutes team punt cover and punt return; Friday—No punting; Saturday—Game.

The following punting program has produced results for us. We start out with stance and work through each phase until it becomes instinctive. Once a boy does exactly the same thing every time he kicks a ball, his punting will be consistent.

Stance: Kicking foot is forward, a little more than heel-toe relationship. Weight is evenly distributed, with good body balance so you can move in any direction. Feet must be parallel, pointing directly at target. Heel of non-kicking foot must remain on ground, or close to it. Both legs are bent slightly at the knees; the body bent forward at the waist. Hands are outstretched with fingers comfortably spread. At no time should the punter stand up.

> SNAP FROM CENTER: As the ball is snapped from the center, the punter steps with the kicking foot. Do not stand still and catch the ball. As you catch the ball, a 6- to 8-inch step is taken with the kicking foot. The center should aim the ball between the upper ankle and knee of the kicking foot—which helps insure the punter staying low.

Holding ball for punt: Support ball in same hand as foot with which you kick (right hand, right foot), laces on top. Right hand should support ball underneath, with middle finger pointing up bottom seam of ball (Figure 1). Guide ball with left hand along left side of ball. Ball should be held slightly lower than waist. Release the ball first with left hand (guide hand). At about the same time that the hands leave the ball, the ball is released just below the waist—and the kicking foot leaves the ground. Nose of ball must be pointed toward the target.

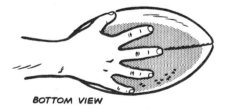

BOTTOM VIEW

Figure 1

> DROPPING THE BALL: This is one of the major keys to your punting game. It must be dropped hundreds of times until the punter can close his eyes, take his steps, and still meet the ball soundly.

Kicking the ball: Never take your eyes off the ball. Kick straight through. Don't swing leg around in front of your body. Person standing behind you should see your right foot over your right shoulder (Figure 2). Left-footed punter would be opposite. If kicking foot ends up over opposite shoulder, you are slicing the ball which takes power away from your kick. Foot must be fully arched and locked at contact of ball.

Figure 2

LEG SNAP AND LOCK: The snap of your leg (speed with which you hit the ball) gives you your power and distance. Leg lock and follow-through gives you height. Snap comes from the speed and power you generate with your kicking foot as you bring it forward from its farthest point back—until it meets the ball and your leg locks and starts on its follow-through. On your follow-through your leg must be locked, knee and ankle.

As for shoe care, it's a good idea to loosen three or four strings on your shoes over the arc to allow freedom of movement. Also, treat bottom of shoe so that the sole is flexible. If leather becomes hard, you cannot arch your foot. There should be no twist in the shoe laces. Tie

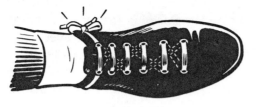

Figure 3

the shoe at side of ankle or in the back (Figure 3) so that you do not kick over knots.

Meeting the ball: A slight wobble on the ball is best—you can get a better roll. A smooth, spinning spiral usually hits on end—no roll or bounce back. The bottom seam of the ball should hit at center of the shoelaces—or cross laces from inside to outside (Figure 4). Use same straight-through kicking arc. Ball will be slightly below the waist at the kick. Heel of non-kicking foot never raises more than ½'' to 1'' off the ground.

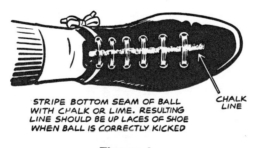

STRIPE BOTTOM SEAM OF BALL WITH CHALK OR LIME. RESULTING LINE SHOULD BE UP LACES OF SHOE WHEN BALL IS CORRECTLY KICKED

CHALK LINE

Figure 4

POST-KICK STEPS: If your kick was properly executed, your feet will be in their original position—and you'll have taken two extra post-kick steps. If your last two steps are to the right or left, you were probably off-balance that way and the ball will go in that direction (Figure 5).

Out-of-bounds kick: Aim the lead foot toward spot you wish to hit. Arch toe down as far as possible. Nose of ball may be held a little

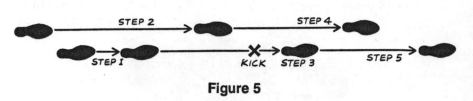

Figure 5

high if you think you may kick into the end zone. Follow-through should be extra high. The ball will not go as far, will not turn over, and may come back toward the kicking team—making ball difficult to field by the opponent.

> PRACTICE: Start practicing from 15 yards back, 15 yards in from the sideline (Figure 6). Use flags or stakes to mark the goal line, 5-yard line, and 10-yard line. Use a different marker to indicate the target where you want the ball to go out-of-bounds.

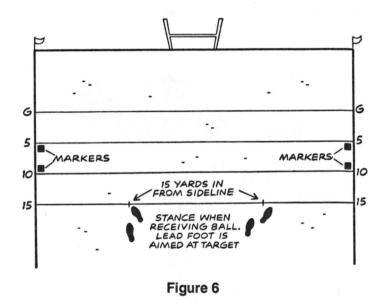

Figure 6

If you have a natural drift to the left, aim your marker a little to the right. If you drift to the right, move marker a little to the left. Kick the ball to go out between the 5- and 10-yard line. After you perfect your kick at 15 yards, move back 10 or 15 yards to the 25- or 30-yard line. Then move back 10 or 15 yards more. Work to perfect the short kicks first.

> TIME BREAKDOWN: You must get your kick away no later than 1-1/2 to 1-3/5 seconds from the time of the snap. On a 35-yard punt, the ball should stay in the air for at least 4 seconds. This gives the linemen almost 6 seconds to cover a 35-yard punt. There will be no return.

21

Mechanics and Drills for "Punch Style" Place-Kicking

by Richard Blaettler

Assistant Football Coach
Richmond (California) High School

Richard Blaettler graduated from San Francisco State in 1962 with a Master's degree in Physical Education. In the years that followed, he coached football at Lowell (San Francisco, Calif.) High School and then went to Springfield (Mass.) College for advanced study during which he coached freshman football. In 1966, he became head junior varsity football coach at Arroyo (San Lorenzo, Calif.) High School. In 1970, he moved to Richmond High School as an assistant varsity football coach. His current duties include defensive coordinator and coaching the offensive line and linebackers.

A mechanical analysis of place-kicking, using the straight-ahead, one-step approach, can be of great help to coaches endeavoring to teach this special skill.

> FIGURE 1: By reducing the basic foot movements to one step, as shown in Figure 1, the place-kicker can make the quickest possible completion of the entire kicking movement.

Three simple movements: The force for the place-kick comes basically from three simple movements:

First, with the place-kicker facing the line of scrimmage, there is the forward or linear movement which starts the body in motion in the direction of the desired flight of the ball. It's best to have the place-kicker in forward motion prior to his foot making contact with the football. The place-kicking technique starts with a step and correct foot placement of the non-kicking foot—and a follow-through with the kicking foot.

> EXAMPLE: For example, a right-footed place-kicker would take a stance in which he would be one step behind the football, with the right or kicking foot ahead of the left or nonkicking foot in a heel-toe relationship.

His body position should be normal and relaxed, and slightly forward during the entire place-kicking movement. The feet are spread apart normally about 4 inches. The distance between the heel and toe and the kicking toe will vary among place-kickers—depending upon

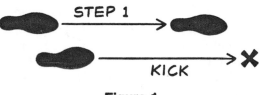

Figure 1

leg length and individual preference. But at all times, it should remain constant for the individual.

The second movement for developing force can be described as a rotary movement of the kicking leg, with the hip joint acting as the center of rotation (axis). The kicking leg is drawn back as the step is taken toward the football. As the stepping or non-kicking foot hits the ground at the end of the step, the kicking leg starts forward.

> NOTE: Rotary motion is characterized by its angular speed and length of the radius of the circle of rotation. Bending the kicking leg gives a shorter radius of rotation and greater velocity. The speed of the lower portion of the kicking leg is greatest when the kicking foot reaches a point directly below the hip.

The third and final source of force is the action of the lower portion of the kicking leg. As the leg is drawn back, it is important that the knee is flexed. The degree to which the knee is flexed will vary with the individual's strength—and the distance the football has to travel. This flexion at the knee permits the leg to move forward with greater angular velocity because of the shortened radius of the total kicking leg. The kicking leg is extended when the kicking toe meets the football. This gives the longest possible lever of radius of rotation—and also the greatest force to the place-kick.

> NOTE: The kicking leg is swung directly in line with the desired flight of the football, and is held at a right or 90° angle to the lower leg so that the full force of the kick will be imparted to the football. The non-kicking foot is placed firmly on the ground, about 6 inches behind and 4 inches to the side of the football—so that the kicking foot will be right in line with the desired direction of flight. The non-kicking foot is also the aiming foot and should be pointed in the direction of flight.

The most important consideration regarding the three basic mechanical movements is that the speed of each member of the body involved in place-kicking be succeedingly faster in movement in order to develop maximum force. The basic approach to the football should never vary—and the football should always be kicked with the same force, regardless of the distance the ball has to travel.